COMPLIMENTS OF

SKYBRIDGE
CAPITAL

WWW.SKYBRIDGECAPITAL.COM

GOODBYE GORDON GEKKO

HOW TO FIND YOUR FORTUNE
WITHOUT LOSING YOUR SOUL

ANTHONY
SCARAMUCCI

WILEY
John Wiley & Sons, Inc.

Published by John Wiley & Sons, Inc., Hoboken, New Jersey.
Published simultaneously in Canada.

For general information on our other products and services or for technical support,
please contact our Customer Care Department within the United States at (800)
762-2974, outside the United States at (317) 572-3993 or fax (317) 572-4002.

Wiley also publishes its books in a variety of electronic formats. Some content that appears
in print may not be available in electronic books. For more information about Wiley
products, visit our web site at www.wiley.com.

ISBN 978-0-470-61954-4

Printed in the United States of America

10 9 8 7 6 5 4 3 2 1

To John F. Iacobucci,
a dear friend who was brave,
dignified, and never lost his faith in
all that is wonderful and special in life.

Contents

Introduction

I met Oliver Stone for the first time in 1987. He doesn't remember it. For a dramatist like me, this is more painful than him saying, "Oh yeah I remember meeting you and hated every minute it of it." I always laugh a little bit about this experience as I pride myself on being able to make a first impression. It may or may not be a good one, but an impression nevertheless.

It was December of that year and he was screening his new movie, *Wall Street*, at the Harvard Square Theatre to a group of second-year Harvard Law School students. I was so excited and got to the theater early. When the movie was over he patiently took questions. He was direct and blunt, but also incredibly warm. Although Oliver never worked on Wall Street, he had a good understanding of it because his dad was a broker and also wrote an investment letter. When he talked about his father, you could see his sentimental side. But throughout the entire Q&A, a consistent theme emerged: Oliver Stone seemed disgusted with greed and thought Gordon Gekko was morally deplorable.

■ ■ ■

It was two months after the October 1987 crash and it seemed like an era was ending. Little did we all know that we were setting up for one of the biggest market runs in history, only to end up in 2008 with the worst financial crisis in 80 years. But in the late 1980s, I was hung up on finding a high-paying, high-status job on Wall Street. Like many of my overachieving peers, I thought it was a ticket out of my middle-class background and the surest way to pay off my school debt. The boom was taking place and Wall Street was being glorified by the media. Despite the market crash, the opportunities for those who landed the big jobs on Wall Street seemed endless. I set my sights on Goldman Sachs and I was lucky enough to get an offer there after my graduation in June 1989—but things did not work out the way I expected.

Essentially, my career started the day I saw *Wall Street*. For many of us who went to work on Wall Street, and who weren't too embarrassed to admit it, that movie had a deep impact on our lives. It was a movie with lines that resonated with us: "Greed is good," "Money never sleeps," "If you're not inside, you're outside!" "I guess I realized that I'm just Bud Fox." It was a movie that had many complex characters, glamour and fancy consumerism, a father-son struggle, and ultimately a taste of redemption and a sacking of evil. It was an iconic movie that marked the beginning, not the end, of an era characterized by all the destructive forces of greed and envy that we as a nation and world are now trying to sort out.

Watching it in the late 1980s, we all took something very different from the film and identified with its different characters, both the good and the bad. Personally, I thought the movie exposed some of the more immoral characters and despicable parts of life on Wall Street. However, even today, people still recite the lines, wear the suspenders, and ultimately try to act like its most unsavory character, Gordon Gekko. Gekko was a fast-talking, high-earning, ruthless, and greedy Wall Street legend whose specialty was manipulating the market and taking over and "wrecking companies." Having made lots of money, he led the high life, which seemingly made some of his illegal actions and self-centered advice justifiable.

I often think of that scene in the original *Wall Street* movie when Bud Fox, the young, ambitious stock broker from Queens, meets the uber-beast Gordon Gekko. As Bud waits outside his idol's office to present him with a box of Cuban cigars for his birthday, he stares at his reflection in the mirror and says "Life all comes down to a few moments; this is one of them." As he walks in and sees the slick Gekko doing business, he is easily seduced by the man's swagger and opulent office. You see, Bud desperately wants to be a part of the inside crowd, get rich quick, and "bag the elephant." Faust with a yellow tie, briefcase, and suspenders, he got sucked into the promise of fame and fortune, and began to break the rules and go down the path of self-destruction and immorality.

Over the past 20 years on the Street, I have done business with many people who wanted to be like Gordon Gekko and actually lived by his motto, "Greed is good." This Wall Street mantra couldn't be further from the truth, yet it is one of the most infamous sentences in Hollywood history. Oliver Stone is a master at composite sketches and designed the sentence. Ivan Boesky, a disgraced arbitrageur, more or less said something like that during the hyperacquisitive 1980s. Why has that sentence had such impact? For starters, it's asymmetric. The word *greed* is a negative word, *is* is a neutral word, and *good* is a positive word. It jars your brain with asymmetry. If Oliver Stone had written in the screenplay "Greed is bad," it would sit just fine with all of us. It would have been conventional and, as such, forgotten. The fact that he had Gekko say, "Greed is good" stuck in our collective craw as a rejection of one of society's basic tenets. It made us think, and made us question our values.

Is greed good? Of course it isn't. Greed—and the desire for money and power—causes good people to make a series of bad decisions until they are no longer considered good. Tempted by fortune, lavish material possessions, and thoughts of an American Express black card, people line up and stand ready to trade in their soul and their values to be "somebody." Most people on Wall Street are by and large good people, but the ones who have traded in their souls for an astronomic paycheck and a multimillion-dollar bonus have won over the media and have made

Wall Street—and those who work there—the new populist punching bag. Some of it is well deserved, but some of it is overdone. Trust me, there are successful people on Wall Street who have done it fairly, with a degree of compassion and generosity. I have met many of those people along the way and have learned a lot from them. And you will learn about a few of them and their lessons if you keep reading.

To me, having ambition, owning a sense of purpose, being a team player, contributing to charities—these are all good. Wrecking companies because you can is not ever going to be good. Sitting as a prop trader and betting on highly leveraged strategies when you have no personal skin in the game is not good. Running a commercial or investment bank and only worrying about your gross pay stub and not the collective welfare of your shareholders, customers, and employees is really not good. Yet some people still think greed is good—even today, after it has caused a global financial crisis that resulted in record-breaking unemployment, a currency crisis, and the loss of confidence in regulatory agencies.

■ ■ ■

I always thought I had at least one book in me—I just wasn't sure if I would have time to write it or whether I would find both clarity and purpose to do so. Then my friend David Molner invited me to a breakfast with Oliver Stone and two of his producers, Ed Pressman and Eric Kopeloff. While discussing the sequel to *Wall Street* over our meal, it became clear to me that I wanted to chronicle my life on Wall Street— the wins and the losses, the rights and the wrongs, the successes and failures, the good mentors and the egotistical colleagues. I wanted to share a voice about Wall Street that isn't often shared, sort of a personal behind-the-scenes view of the good and the bad and the lessons learned. After our meeting, I became one of the technical advisers on the *Wall Street* sequel, *Wall Street: Money Never Sleeps* and decided to write this book. Both have been a fantastic learning experience and I had a great time doing them.

Twenty-three years since the release of the first film, the new movie is about wilder excess and even crazier personalities. We now face even greater challenges, temptations, and roadblocks that consequently accompany our professional ambitions and personal decisions. It's time to make serious choices about how we are going to define ourselves. This is a story about those definitions, personal and otherwise.

Chapter 1

Ambition
Ego versus the Egomaniac

Some people grow, other people swell. You'd better figure out who you are.

—*John Weinberg,*
Senior partner and chairman,
Goldman Sachs, 1976–1990

We never really know how it is going to end up. One day a community organizer, the next day president. Life twists and turns with only one real certainty: All of us will be forced to accept change and adapt. We all have varying degrees of ambition but no matter what level you have, things will likely not go exactly the way you want them to.

Ambition usually starts where most Disney movies end—you know, right at the happily ever after. We all secretly hope for this. But think about it for a minute—Disney stories are brutal. Bambi loses a parent; Cinderella has a wicked stepmother; Snow White is stuck with seven short, fat guys, and on and on. It doesn't matter that we all think in our youth that we are going to get everything we want and life will work out perfectly for us. It never does.

So what happens when the "happily" gets ripped out of the "ever after?" Do you think Lehman Brothers CEO Dick Fuld or Merrill Lynch chief John Thain thought 2008 would destroy their careers? Did the management team at Goldman Sachs expect to go from respected and revered to respected and mostly reviled? They are now the piñata for greed and ambition run amok. Should they be? It doesn't matter. Through it all, the billboard message from the 2008 economic debacle: Nothing—especially money—lasts forever. Shit happens.

Sure, money is a great thing and fun to have. Life without money is in most cases worse than life with it. But I bet the people who have been tossed around in the latest economic calamity would trade some of their wealth for a reputation restoration. We are not talking about the criminals here; we'll get to them in another chapter. What I'm talking about is the classic hubris that comes right before some dude comes crashing down—alone in his surprise—from his pedestal.

The arc of ambition moves in the direction that it wants to. Sure, we can try to guide it through hard work and bold decisions, but secretly so much of it is out of our hands.

Essentially, we have no idea of where our life will end up.

Sandy Weill—the Wall Street legend who rose, fell, rose, and fell again—often said: "I prepare for the worst, and pray for the best." Similarly, in the book *True North* (Jossey-Bass, 2007), authors Bill George and Peter E. Sims interviewed leaders older than 40. None of them wound up where they thought they would. Not one.

Stuff happens. Never have truer words been spoken. It is up to us to approach life with the right attitude and positively react, not letting changes diminish our spirit or initiative, or damage our personal reputation. If we keep our values intact we will be fine regardless of what happens. But we always have to expect the unexpected.

Speaking of our values, we all hear the same childhood stories, listen to the same lessons in school on goodness. Aesop. Greek Mythology. Boy Scout and Girl Scout ethics guidebooks. Sunday school lessons. We get doused in the values bath. Be good to each other, our neighbors, friends, and family. The trouble is that when we are on the ascent of Mount Getting It All, we get blinded by our own ambition, and consequently start to rationalize our thinking and start to make very big mistakes. Like exercise and proper eating, we have to remind ourselves of what makes us honest, true, and fair. Doing so will keep us out of Gekkoland, the land where we compromise our morals and integrity in exchange for money and status.

This isn't always possible, and this isn't a self-help book, just a realistic assessment of some of the common struggles we encounter and ways in which we can overcome them. As you try to build your fortune, you are going to get tossed to the floor. How you get up and react to the things that happen to you will make all the difference. Sure, your life may not end up the way you secretly planned or expected it to, but you will still be able to find your fortune as long as you stick to your principles and build a circle of competence.

■ ■ ■

Here's a confession: I coasted until I was about 18.

I wanted to play sports, be popular, tool around the Long Island suburbs in my red 1979 Camaro Berlinetta, go out on dates, and breeze through school. I did okay—ranked about 124 out of 455 kids in my class. My adolescence was best described by two words: dissimulated and desultory. I was having a great time but I wasn't really having a *fulfilling* great time.

I was a varsity athlete, and the captain and quarterback on the football team. The scouting report on me was: Short, but strong; no real arm strength but clever and confident on the field; can read the defense, and is capable of calling plays and audibles.

I was cut from Italian genes, not the kind you wear but the stuff that you landed with at Ellis Island. I had brown hair, brown eyes, and a stocky build, always quick with a smile and a wisecrack. Gold chains, too. It was a hollow and shallow existence, and even as a teenager I kind of knew it.

I took dance lessons; it was the age of *Saturday Night Fever* and I wanted to make sure I knew all of the moves on the dance floor. I had my hair cut by guys named Hugo and Marcello. I got away with stuff, and the more I got away with the more I pushed. No drugs or alcohol—I was one of the few in my class who avoided it, but that didn't make me any less of a wise guy.

I needed teenage attention, from girls, my teammates, and, of course, my teachers. I was the student body president. I pushed people and probably suffered from Tourette's syndrome. If it was in my head, I was likely going to say it, especially if it was going to get a laugh. I played for laughs. I was Ferris Bueller. My goal was to always find a way to talk myself out of the principal's office.

A switch flipped for me when it came time to pick a college. My mom and dad never went to college. They are second-generation Italian-Americans without college degrees but they were hell-bent on me getting one.

My dad grew up in the Wilkes-Barre/Scranton area of Pennsylvania, where they film *The Office* today. Steve Carell didn't live there back then, but Irish, Welsh, and Italian immigrants did. It was loaded with coal miners and small-time industrialists. It was a Depression-era small town and there was poverty and hardship.

My dad graduated from Plains High School in Plains, Pennsylvania, in 1953. As soon as he could, he left that town and followed his older brother to Port Washington, New York, where I grew up. He enlisted in the army, was stationed in Louisiana, and thankfully never got shipped out to Korea. He was from Northern Italian descent, with a small build like me and lighter than my mom, who descended from Southern Italian stock. He started as a laborer and worked at the same construction company for 42 years, eventually becoming its president. He was never afraid of hard work and was extremely intent upon making sure that my siblings and I never feared it either.

My mom grew up in Port Washington, where she met my dad and married him in 1957. She was petite, and when she was young, people said she looked like Natalie Wood (something she reminded us of just about every day). She raised us, made the beds, did the laundry, cooked for us, and handled every other detail of our home. It sounds classic and stereotypical but she is far from that. She prides herself in having a sense of fashion and to this day is strongly opinionated. She is great in math and has a keen ability to determine someone's character. She's also very observant and not afraid to be herself.

Growing up, we were never in want for anything, especially good food, but it was a financial sacrifice for my parents to give my siblings and me a formal education. That sort of woke me up. How could I let my folks down? I was popular, president of the school, a varsity athlete, and tested well enough . . . I just wasn't operating at my full throttle. I was coasting through the classes, all the while fidgeting and daydreaming. It was obvious to everyone around me.

One of my math teachers even wrote in my high school yearbook that I would spend my whole life trying to put a gallon of water into a one-quart bottle. He was dead wrong in only seeing a quart of capacity in me, but he was right on the money about trying to do too much. I still haven't figured out that one.

When it came time for me to pick a college, my dad had a close friend by the name of Billy Tomasso, a Tufts graduate and generous alum. My grades—probably because of all that tooling around in the Camaro— weren't strong enough to get into Tufts without a little help. Luckily, Billy saw something in me and set up a meeting with Sol Gittleman, a scholar and at the time the school's provost.

In November 1981, I took the Eastern Airlines shuttle to Boston from New York to visit with Sol. That was the start of an unlikely alliance between an overgrown, overachieving Jewish man from New Jersey and an undergrown, underachieving Italian kid from Long Island. The conversation, as best I can remember, went something like this:

"Please Sol, help me get into Tufts. If you do, I won't let you down."

"If I do, you have to promise you will take my Yiddish Literature course."

And so I did, and I learned the difference between a *shaygits* and a *shiksa*, among many other things. Thanks, Sol. (If you don't know the difference and want to learn it, you will have to keep reading.) I also realized that I had to gear up and convert whatever talent I had into a singular purpose or be resigned to a life that came up short of satisfaction and true happiness. Tooling around in the Camaro was no longer an option. Don't get me wrong, the power booster in the car that enhanced the stereo system was great—but there was more to life. It didn't feel right.

I always liked to read, and I knew that I had to try to be something different to break out of the middle-class band that I was in. The American Dream lives and I wanted to experience it. So I promised myself that I would be serious. The days of playing hard and working easy were ending.

Needless to say, my brother and I were lucky that we happened to go to a world-class university, with an enlightened faculty and a tight student-to-professor ratio. I became close to several faculty members in addition to Sol, including my classics professor, John Zarker, and my economics professor, Dan Ounjian. These were people who put their students first and pushed people with high expectations and standards. The love I have for Tufts has no bounds because the people there took a chance on a very immature and unproven kid—me—and the education that I received not only benefited my intellectual capacity but also my soul.

In retrospect, I am not sure what woke me up. If I had to guess, it was mostly the fear of not seeing where my potential could take me. We have this common struggle: How much torque and drive are we going to apply to life? How will we handle the bumps that we hit?

The possibilities of being happy and satisfied also drove me. Fun comes in many varieties, but the sort of fun that I was having was always unsatisfying. You have to work hard and play hard. I have never been one for moderation. Balance is the key, just not for me. If you are going to do something, take it to an extreme. Just remember that play is always way more satisfying *after* work—not before.

It's similar to what President Barack Obama wrote in *Dreams from My Father* (Three Rivers Press, 1995, 2004): If the bell didn't ring in his head to get serious, history was about to pass him by. Apparently, his bell rang and he became a historic figure. We were in law school together for one year. The history part wasn't ever in my mind— I wonder if it was in his. Regardless, the bell rang and I answered it.

It's never too late. If it hasn't rung for you yet, it's time to force it into happening. You already know. Back then, I knew. If you aren't where you want to be, gear up and work at making it better. You can give up in the coffin. If you are breathing, the time is now.

■■■

There's a list of clichés that others often repeat: Answer the call. Dare to dream. Be audacious. Here are mine:

- Pain in life comes from a lot of different things—the goal is not to self-inflict it.
- Nothing is more soul-crushing than the regret that follows a dream denied due to a lack of effort.
- Failure, save for a trek up Everest or a space mission, isn't a problem if the attempt is whole-hearted.
- Within the simple, sincere pursuit of dreams there is something special and wonderful, no matter the outcome.

We need to appreciate the obstacles, embrace them. Too often we lament and whine. Someone doesn't do what we expect. Our assumptions confront reality and reality wins. There are just so many things to distract and deter us. Even our own fears of success get in the way. That's right—most of us quietly fear it. Suppose we get everything we want and we still aren't happy—then what? Also, with success comes responsibility. People start leaning on you and want to be lifted. So all of this needs to be dealt with.

When I started college, I was ready to give it my all. My ambition was able to burst through all of these obstacles. I was going to make an effort, whether I failed or succeeded. I hunkered down and, after countless late nights of studying and intense work, graduated near the top of my class at Tufts (no more middling class-ranks for me), got a degree from Harvard Law School, went on to Goldman Sachs, and then set off on my own to pursue my passion: becoming an entrepreneur and starting my own company.

The hedge fund I started with Andrew K. Boszhardt Jr., called Oscar Capital, was successful enough that Neuberger Berman, a publicly traded money management firm, purchased it in 2001 and I became close personal friends with the senior executives there, Jeff Lane and Bob Matza. Neuberger was sold to Lehman Brothers in October 2003. It was a lucky sort of double dip. In 2005, I left Lehman and launched another company, SkyBridge Capital, a money management business dedicated to helping money managers go out on their own. Along the way I have made some money.

More importantly, though, I have learned from my parents and tycoons, my uncles and professors, politicians and my grandmother— and from those lessons built a framework for life that adds up to more than a list of achievements, well beyond a paycheck, and a far higher calling than the opinions of others.

■■■

I have worked on Wall Street for 20 years. Pariah Land.

I would love to say that I work on Wall Street but have never really been a part of it. But I am.

I am a Wall Street hump. I am not sure why. Just a series of choices I made at the time that added up. However, I want to be a special one, if there is such a thing.

Do you remember Sherman McCoy? He was the infamous protagonist of Tom Wolfe's classic *The Bonfire of the Vanities*. Sherman was a leading New York City bond trader and a self-regarded "Master of the Universe" on Wall Street who egotistically believed that he was entitled to his annual million-dollar salary, penthouse, sports cars, designer suits, and mistress. These Masters of the Universe referred to their wives as either Lemon Tarts (the new, second trophy wife) or social X-rays (the older, waif-thin first wife hanging on by a thread). Essentially, McCoy was a symbol of the wretched excesses of the Eighties. Yet he believed that he only *worked* on Wall Street, that he wasn't *part* of it, it wouldn't change him, and he was only using it to make money. Yeah right, he was the North Star of Wall Street.

You see, we all like to be in denial and like to think of ourselves above the masses. How many of us think we are average or below average? How many of us think we are greedy, selfish, arrogant bastards? Yet there is no escaping reality, and the truth doesn't lie.

It seems that many people currently have a poor image of Wall Street and the people who work on it. Since the financial meltdown, people around Wall Street complain they've gotten a bum rap in the press, been beaten up by politicians, and felt the backlash from Main Street. Well, take a look around, boys—it didn't happen by accident. It was an accumulation of a lot of greedy actions. Greed, self-interest, and lack of caring are widespread on the Street. It is unfortunate because a lot of good and philanthropy have come from the world of finance, which I will get to later in the book. Yet we still see the rogues, the thieves, and the incessant, self-centered greed. We may laugh at the Gekko and McCoy stereotypes, but that perception has now become reality.

Generally, I live by the "3 percent" theory. Three percent of the people are raw evil—spawn of Lucifer, Hitler, and Stalin. Three percent of the people are pure good—the Kings, the Mandelas, the John Paul IIs, the Mother Teresas. Everyone else is in between. On a planet of 6.7 billion people, having 210 million dark princes and princesses can lead to a lot of trouble. There are many people who stand ready to wear explosive underpants.

On Wall Street, we unfortunately have the "5 and 1" rule: 5 percent are bad, 1 percent are good. Most are in between—slanted toward the good side, but there are just too many bad people even though they are in the minority. They have hurt the industry. Their transparent avarice and arrogance converts into superiority and entitlement as they succeed. The other folks see it and despise it. It is up to us—the people who work in this industry—to figure out a way to change all of these negative perceptions and say goodbye to Gordon Gekko forever. What better way to do so than to learn firsthand from the many experiences, mistakes, mentors, and lessons I've had on (and off) the Street?

■ ■ ■

Some of the most profound lessons of my life came during my time as a trainee at Goldman Sachs in the late 1980s. These days, the firm is frequently vilified as one of the causes of the financial meltdown or one that profits from its connections and influence in governments around the world. The new conspiracy theories are around "Government Sachs." That's one view that I don't share. I just think the firm has gone over its skis into the arrogance territory. People sense it and every move is now met with a comment. When I was there, it was not the "great vampire squid" sucking the life out of the global economy, and it isn't that today, either.

The firm plays to win, and it attracts the best and brightest, with bosses smart enough to motivate and train them. The firm is an exceptional place, and for me it was the training ground and the foundation of my inclusion and success on Wall Street.

In a span of about 20 years, Goldman would launch the careers of two U.S. Treasury secretaries, two national economic advisers, an Export-Import Bank head, a U.S. Trade representative, a Democratic National Committee (DNC) finance chair, a future ambassador to Switzerland, the current ambassador to Germany, a future New York Fed president, a governor of New Jersey (and before that, a senator), a White House chief of staff, and a dozen of the world's best hedge fund managers. The men who built the firm into a Wall Street powerhouse are the ones who trained me.

In 1989, I sat there, eager to be initiated into the Goldman way, and heard John Weinberg, the legendary former CEO and chairman of the firm, say simply: "Some people grow, other people swell. You'd better figure out who you are." That was the core of the Goldman pedigree. Individual ambitions had to be sublimated to the mission of the group. Everyone there was smart, talented, and filled with potential. The key was keeping everyone working for each other, not having each boy genius's ego and ambitions swell to crowd out his colleagues.

At Goldman, we proudly saw Wall Street as a place where traders, brokers, and bankers were cowboys armed with two six-shooters. The difference was that at other firms a guy had one gun aimed at the competition and one aimed at the guy next to him; at Goldman we had both pointed at our rivals. The goal was to diminish corporate infighting as much as possible. Don't focus on competing with each other; focus on profits and partnering with each other. It was rare then, and it's even more unique now.

Over the past two decades, it's become clear that sublimating the self to almost anything else is a tough sell not only on Wall Street but on Main Street, too. But even back then I noticed that not everyone bought into the ideas Weinberg and the other Goldman lions were trying to pass along. I just didn't realize that the abandonment of teamwork and the supremacy of the individual's goals would become a staple of the entire American culture before long.

The ambitions of the individual manifested themselves in the worst possible way. They showed up in the huge paychecks executives gave to themselves, in runaway consumer spending fueled by debt, and in a culture obsessed with the fulfillment of possessions, and possessing. As a nation, we chased empty dreams for the wrong reasons: to create a perception of our well-being to the outside world, to soothe deep-rooted status anxiety, and to inflate our sense of self. A generation of me-first.

It started out in the 1960s, with long hair and rebellion. The 1970s, the sexual revolution. The 1980s, consumption and pasta al dente. The 1990s and 2000s, the years of delaying sacrifice and expanding consumption. We developed a group of politicians who have consistently made decisions based on their temporary survival at the cost of their permanent legacy and that of the society. From the greatest generation, who made sacrifices to defeat the Nazis, to the worst generation, who are squandering America's treasure.

Does this all sound sanctimonious? I didn't mean it to be—I was right in there with everyone else, chasing possessions and trying to improve my perceived social status. It's what most of us do, and almost all of us who work on Wall Street. We chase and we become absorbed, and if we are not careful, we make the mistake of Bud Fox in *Wall Street*: We give ourselves up to be part of the inside crowd. We do the wrong things, go against our values, and allow greed to trump wisdom. The wanting to feel in, needed, special, relevant.

Again, ambition is not bad, nor is it new. But our ability to express it has grown exponentially in the past two decades, even as our capacity to understand and manage it seems to have evaporated. I have seen this happen among a few of my bosses, colleagues, and clients, and I have spent no small amount of time keeping an eye on my own ambition, as well.

But I digress.

In 1989, I worked in Goldman's Investment Banking Division, the elite of the elite. By 1994, I was in its private wealth division, the unit that serviced the investment needs of the super-rich. My office was on a floor that was home to no fewer than 35 millionaires. Yet, on that one floor—and Goldman probably had 10 more like it—there was enough griping and dissatisfaction around me that I began to call my colleagues "The Miserable Millionaires Club." A rich complainer isn't an oxymoron, just a moron.

It's known as the Neighbor Effect. William Bernstein, in his 2004 book *Birth of Plenty* (McGraw-Hill), explains the phenomenon well: "Absolute wealth matters less than the wealth relative to your neighbors. . . . Or as more tartly put by H. L. Mencken, a wealthy man is one who earns more than his wife's brother-in-law." There is also something in suburban America called *dumpster envy*. One's house is perfectly fine and satisfying until the neighbor drops the dumpster off and begins renovating. People can be rich but still unhappy as long as they have people near them who appear richer. So crazy, but a reality that we deal with.

I was amazed to see that for most Goldman guys, it wasn't enough to be a millionaire; in their social circle or work circle, they had to be king of the jungle. To them, being a millionaire wasn't enough if they hadn't won prestigious partner status at the firm. They saw themselves as merely working stiffs, like the kid behind the counter at Dunkin' Donuts or a bank teller in the Bronx, but with better cars and shiny cuff links. They were rich by anyone's definition except their own. A cop, a schoolteacher, even most doctors and lawyers would have been satisfied with half the money and options that it brought. Wall Street millionaires quickly forget how lucky they are and how high they've climbed up the food chain of money. Most people would be grateful and happy with far less. Yet, as humans, we have a tendency to get to a place that we never really even dreamed of and still find our discontentment there.

■■■

It seemed insane to me, but by 1995 I had joined the club of millionaires, after six short years. Then I got it. Getting to one level means the next step should be accessible, too, right? The question that began to gnaw at me was: "I am just as smart as that guy. Why is he doing better?"

It's a shallow question, admittedly, but one that most of us (save for the rare missionary, NFL offensive lineman, and a handful of Tibetan monks) have asked. And it's one that few will confess to because it exposes all of our insecurities and egotistical tendencies to the world.

Yet there is nothing more infuriating than watching someone who you think is dumber than you getting rich. The whole Internet bubble was created by this. You mean the imbecile next door became a millionaire buying Yahoo!? I want my chance to become rich, too; he is no smarter than me . . . and hence the bubble and mania starts. None of us are saints, and even the most sublime among us have petty competitive drives and jealousies. It is Darwinism applied to individuals instead of to gene pools and species.

The true secret to controlling this overambition is first recognizing these feelings and then figuring out a positive and transformational way to deal with them. The best among us can drop our envy and celebrate the successes of our friends. What a gift to teach children: Celebrate the successes of your friends. Drop the atavistic social Darwinism and become sublime. Be joyful for the joy of others.

We haven't been able to do that as a culture, but each of us every day can try to do it as individuals. I am convinced many of the problems that precipitated the great economic crisis of 2008 sprang from jealousy, which caused us to temporarily lose our ability, and our desire, to control. While the Wall Street bosses have been publicly flogged during televised Congressional hearings, they are not the only culprits. Sure, on Wall Street unchecked ego and boundless ambition led to untenable risks. Let's not forget, though, that at the same time, Main Street was buying into the advertising message of a must-have lifestyle and ran consumer debt to its highest level ever.

Let's start with where Wall Street's ambition went wrong. Here's the conversation inside of the head of a corporate titan:

> "Wow, I am the CEO of Schlehman and I just made $10 million. That makes me feel awesome."
> "What? The CEO of Schmoldman made $26 million? How is that possible? I have to find a way to overtake that guy."

Now add three or four more Gordon Gekkos to the equation. They all simultaneously take on more risk in pursuit of more rewards because, after all, that's how they and the world gauge their value.

That value, naturally, has to be more than everyone else's. More risk leads to more reward, for a while; then it melts into instability. And then comes the crash.

The hedge fund guys compounded this issue and made it worse for everyone else. They were making so much money that the average Wall Street CEO couldn't compete. Some hedge fund guys were making hundreds of millions and the media was celebrating this. So what happened? The Wall Street titans petitioned the regulators to take their leverage up from 20:1 to 34:1. How else were they going to compete with the hedge fund guys for Hamptons real estate or contemporary art at Sotheby's? They turned their businesses into large casinos so they could one-up each other.

For instance, it is just implausible to me that John Weinberg or John Whitehead, who co-managed Goldman and wrote its 14 business principles, would have bet the ranch. They both fought in World War II and witnessed the Great Depression as kids. They didn't have the same expectations about life and were willing to make sacrifices. But when the Wall Street firms went public it became easier for CEOs to take risks with other people's money. This is still something that troubles Alan Greenspan. He thought the modern CEO and management team of these large banks owned enough shares in their businesses that they would not put themselves (or their portfolio) in harm's way; however, the once-perceived "truest wise man of finance" made faulty assumptions, which he now must admit. In 2008 testimony, former Fed Chairman Greenspan said:

I made a mistake in presuming that the self-interest of organizations, specifically banks and others, was capable of protecting their own shareholders and the equity in the firms, and it has been my experience, having worked both as a regulator for 18 years and similar quantities in the private sector, especially 10 years at a major international bank, that the loan officers of those institutions knew far more about the risks involved and the people to whom they lent money than I saw even our best regulators at the Fed capable of doing. So the problem here is something which looked to be a very solid edifice and indeed a critical pillar to market competition, and free markets did break down and I think that shocked me. I still do not fully understand why it happened, and obviously, to the extent that I figure out where it happened and why, I will change my views. As the facts change, I will change.

Translation: I can't believe these bankers, ratings agencies, and buyers could be that greedy, greedy enough to blow themselves up.

And it doesn't stop in the executive suites. No one is immune to the lure and the toxicity of the greed. It's something we all have in common. Each of us, in a smaller, less dramatic way, did some of the same things. Overmortgaged our houses. Took on excessive debt.

The baby boomer generation is especially guilty of this sin. When we do something, we go big—really big. We went from the greatest generation, those who fought in World War II, to the generation of greed and envy. Our problem: We swelled, didn't grow—unless you want to count our combined fatness. As a group we thought nothing of pushing for more and more for ourselves.

Our internal voices now sound something like this:

"My career should be fun. I shouldn't have to sacrifice much."

"Wait, that's a sweeeeet BMW SUV. How much? *That* much?!"

"Hmmm, that refinancing deal sounds good. I can handle a second mortgage. I'll take some cash out. I can always sell this house for more in a few years when it's worth twice what it is now."

"Ka-ching! I'm goin' to Disneyworld!"

But wait—there's more.

We expect our marriages to be like sitcom TV, but far more Huxtable than Bundy. Our kids should be high-achieving, with perfect SATs, be able to act and to play a musical instrument, and have worked on a world-saving charity—before high school graduation. As a result of this grand ambition, we boomers didn't just give the world a simple recession—we produced the mother of all meltdowns.

The sense of self-entitlement and overambition has been nurtured by corporate America's advertising agenda. "Without our product, you just aren't living." Whether it's a cooler-than-thou iPhone, a sporty Mercedes with a ride rivaling your best orgasm, or a mutual fund that far surpasses the market's performance, life is about being better and checking off achievements—personal, professional, and material. The food industry has messaged to us a feeling of dissatisfaction unless we are eating during every major moment of our life and most minor ones, too, like when we're plopped on the couch watching television. You can have it all. Our political class is about overpromising the electorate that they can have all the services they want but don't want to pay for. Is it any wonder that we are walking around fat and punch-drunk from our overleveraged hangover?

Face it: We are all vulnerable to these vices. We now need to stop the insanity and make better choices. Be willing to make some sacrifices so that future generations can benefit.

Be practical and wary. Give yourself an annual ambition checkup. Make sure you are still behaving consistently with your values and not thrown off by the greed-and-envy downward cycle.

Watch *Mad Men*. They figured it out and drank lunchtime martinis, too.

■ ■ ■

Most of what is shoveled toward us is shrewdly aimed at the simple truth that we are biologically wired to compete with each other. We have impulses and ambitions that make us want to be the best. What's great about us is the innovation and the push toward more opportunity—the boldness, the dreaming, and then the doing. But we need to keep it in check or we risk turning into egomaniacs.

We're all a bit familiar with Darwin's theories about survival of the fittest and natural selection. An animal that runs faster than others is more likely to catch its prey, or escape from its enemies, and live to pass along its genes. Today we don't have to compete with other species for food, shelter, and safety, so the battle for survival plays out between people. The smartest, strongest, and most aggressive get the good stuff—including the possibility of reproducing more often. In many animal species, there's competition for mates and, by extension, for the chance to reproduce. Antelope have their unique way of measuring the best mates, and so do people. Unfortunately, too often we have come to believe that the winning qualities include expensive cars, real estate, and fancy vacations.

That seems silly, but it's merely the modern manifestation of the instinct we all have to survive and to reproduce. In the early days of human development there weren't many options or ways to live in the middle. You were predator or prey. That's how ambition, unchecked, can make the world appear. If you're not the best, the top, the richest, you're nothing—even a member of the Miserable Millionaires Club can feel irrelevant. There is nothing worse than that feeling!

These are animalistic or atavistic impulses. Nasty stuff. We've all heard the old saying, "It isn't enough for me to succeed; others must fail." In other words, we get pleasure from other people's pain and pain from their pleasure. That mind-set—what Sol Gittleman called *schadenfreude*—is easier to adopt these days simply because we are less dependent on each other and are constantly competing with one another to have the biggest houses, smartest children, highest bonus, and most vacation homes. All of this makes our worst instincts harder to control.

The challenge for all of us is to rise above these animal impulses; our human evolution should have left those behind by now. That higher self should recognize that there is enough money and enough of all the things it buys for all of us. In 1974, Henry Kissinger said at a UN conference on food and hunger that in 10 years no one on the planet would go hungry, yet a billion people still go to bed hungry 36 years later. Who cares if someone has more (or a little less) as long as they haven't taken it from you? A higher self would express happiness—real happiness—in the success of a colleague or a friend. No tinge of envy, just joy. Why is this so hard?

The worst part of the human spirit is when we can't simply accept another person's success or be comfortable with our own position in the world. It's a status fever. How am I perceived? Am I hanging with the right crowd? Do I belong to the right clubs? It is a competition in the art world, the business world, among our children, and just about everywhere else. Who's looking at me, and how am I doing? Enough of me talking about me—what do *you* think of me? We all in varying ways suffer from it.

■ ■ ■

After two decades of operating in corporate America and as an entrepreneur, I've begun to diagnose strains of this disease of the ego, this virulent strain of ambition. I have tried to inoculate myself from some of them, but oftentimes I have been sucked right in.

Here are some of the most common:

- **The Envyne Flu.** This is sort of like the swine flu. It comes from pigs. First you start out as a capitalist and then you become a capitalist pig. The overfeeding at the trough causes the syndrome. Your wealth accumulates but so does your relative dissatisfaction. It hurts and causes yearning. If you catch this disease and take no steps to push for a cure, it will have disastrous consequences. For envy is unquenchable. It is the green-eyed monster that ultimately eats itself. Victims feel they never have enough. There is always someone out there who has something just slightly (or way) better than the diseased. It is a sad sort of ailment, too. For the person who has envyne flu can never, ever, really be truly happy for another. The only known cure is massive amounts of generosity. If this doesn't drive the victim crazy it has the potential to alleviate most of the symptoms.

- **The 7–10 Verbal Split Habit.** This is the most fun of the ego-maniac afflictions. This is the "put others down to make yourself feel better" syndrome. Going negative. In bowling, a 7–10 split occurs when the far back left pin is smashed into the far right back pin to create a spare. This is very difficult in bowling and requires a lot of practice. Yet this is quite easy to do verbally and happens all the time. The typical 7–10 split in life goes like this: Three people involved—Dick, Rob, and Joe. Dick says to Rob, "Joe thinks you are a jerk and have bad work habits." *Bam*! Well done. Now Rob dislikes Joe even though Dick is the instigator.

  I worked in two very large organizations (Goldman and Lehman), a medium organization (Neuberger Berman), and two small organizations that I had a hand in helping launch (Oscar and SkyBridge). Let me tell you, this happens all the time in places of all sizes. I thought, when I was at Goldman, that when I left I would create the perfect organization. Silly me. Have people, will have backbiting.

  The 7–10 split is sort of silly but very effective. The person doing it is trying to rile others and to create divisions on the road to their own personal advancement. "Joe, Jim doesn't think you are smart enough." "Rachel, Ellen was saying bad things about you to our boss, Peter." It's classic infighting and slighting. It's done to create discord and it's done when people are trying to compete and think about things in a win-lose sort of way. You have probably done it, at least if you work somewhere. And if you don't work somewhere you probably did it to someone socially. I have done it. It is part of the human condition.

  Stop doing it. Do your best to avoid it. Don't partake in it. Nothing poisons a group and sets people against each other more than the 7–10 verbal split. It can hurt business, but more importantly it hurts people. Keep your negative emotions to yourself, and if you are at the workplace, think like an owner and ask yourself: Would the boss want to see this happening? What if my boss heard me creating this insidious gossip? Act like the boss is within earshot—or better yet, the person who you are throwing under the bus. This will lead to more harmony and it will also put you ahead of the crowd. I am not calling for a lack of honesty and evaluation in the workplace, but there is a time and appropriate place for it. Be wise, use your discretion, and it will pay off both socially and professionally.

- **The Windex Disorder.** We all have seen the clear signs of this horrific condition. You are at a cocktail party, a book party, or a charity reception. Midway through a harmless conversation over mini crab cakes, you notice the other person isn't really listening to you. His eyes are dancing over your shoulder, darting to cover the rest of the room. He is Windexing you: Your face is like a sheet of glass upon which he will spray Windex and wipe you clean so he can look past you to someone more important or influential with whom to mingle. The Windexer is a social-climbing, status-conscious, status-anxious sort who shows up at a cocktail party with the goal of always trading up to a better conversation. Never, ever let it be you. Never. Ever. Has it been me? I have Windexed my share of people and have been Windexed, but I am a recovering Windexer now.

  There is something good about the Windexers, though. They teach a valuable lesson: that it's always better to relax and enjoy a party than to bring your Windex and a roll of paper towels.

- **The Island of Elba Syndrome.** When Emperor Napoleon was exiled to Elba, he brooded and plotted his comeback. When he made it back and conquered the Bourbons, he rewarded those who had come to see him while he was sent away. Often when friends lose a job or have a personal setback, they become radioactive to the circles in which they once traveled. The partner/colleague always has a precipitous drop in his obsequious voice mails the day he announces his retirement. Years ago, one of my friends was ousted in the wake of corporate infighting. His phone stopped ringing and he quickly discovered who his friends really were after he was pulled off the corporate power grid. Few people called or wrote. I made sure to drop by.

In corporate life, you may not want to be seen as the ally of someone who screwed up an account or came out on the wrong end of office politics. It'll reflect badly upon you. That's exactly the wrong way to think, especially if that person was your friend.

At some point, we all find ourselves on the wrong end of a deal. Who among Dick Fuld's colleagues are bringing him donuts or are paying him respect the way they did when he strode the 31st floor at Lehman's global headquarters? The side of you that's advising you to stay away from once-close friends or colleagues is the same part of you that is anxious about your own place in the world.

Again, it's time to observe and overcome. Be the friend who shows up with the donuts and reassurance. Not only will your friend appreciate it, but if he is capable and resilient he will rise again . . . and you'll be there with him. Most people in that situation do not forget the kindness showed when they were vulnerable and had little else but their friendship to offer.

- **The Ego Wall Affliction.** Remember the scene in the first *Wall Street* movie, where the young Bud Fox walks into Gordon Gekko's office? Amidst Gekko's egomaniacal appearance and slick talk is an enormous suite full of priceless artwork, the latest gadgets, and opulent furniture.

  Spend enough time on Wall Street, or in any other business, and more than likely you will enter a Gekko-like egomaniac's office—full of pictures of him with famous people and seemingly invaluable artwork—that reflects first and foremost a spasm of self-congratulation. It just screams, "Hey, look at me, I'm a stud!"

  In March 1999, a Goldman colleague and I had the opportunity to visit a prominent Wall Street leader. In his office, I was met with the mother of all ego walls. It wasn't enough to have every famous person and politician who this person thought was smart adorning the wall behind his desk. This whole exercise meant a lot to the titan.

You could tell that he had strategically placed—no doubt after investing much time, thought, and contemplation—the magazine covers that over the years his visage had graced.

What is the affect this sort of monument has on most people? I would guess that the typical person would be awed. Why else would someone put the ego wall up if he didn't want that kind of response?

The ego wall owner is trying to say, quite simply: "Look at me. There is evidence in my office that I am a mover and shaker. I have the best of the best surrounding me, which makes me one of them. Right? I mean, I am the best, right?" That leaves the visitor feeling insignificant in its—and his—shadow.

The ego wall I saw during that 1999 visit was special. Someone had spent hours and hours thinking about what was going up there and how it was going to be placed. The attention to detail was astonishing. The best picture with the best magazine title, with the best byline, was square in the middle of the wall.

We had our meeting (sans photographers, so I guess we weren't worthy of having our picture taken), and as my partner and I were leaving the building, he asked, "So, what did you think?"

"Well for starters, we will never do business with this guy—we aren't important enough," I said. "And I don't know who and I don't know where or when, but some girl at some point in his life asked, 'Is it in yet?'" We laughed and went on with our lives and our business.

If there is a moral to the story, it is to be humble. Put up pictures of your kids, or your family. That's not to say that if you have some celebrity photos you can't sprinkle them in, but there should be a little bit of a story behind them. Celebrate your life; I am not saying be low key, just laugh about it a little. No matter the accolade or the triumph, we share a lot in common with the weakest among us. We carry most of the same emotions. The people who visit your office—your guests—are the important ones. The place where you greet them should be built around making them feel welcome and equal, not intimidated.

■■■

We are all tempted by overambition, greed, and the desire to be viewed by our peers as peerless. That sounds a lot like an ego wall to me. Or maybe like a huge desk that keeps four feet between you and a visitor. Or the need to put up more Christmas lights than your long-time next-door neighbor.

Those impulses, while natural, actually go against our most central need to guarantee our individual happiness and long-term success. Unless we can tame the animal in us, we lose our humanity and our ability to find our fortune without losing our soul. We need to control the yearning and be satisfied with what we have and what we do. But if you have the confidence to exude such a sense of purpose, how can you keep your ego in check as you are achieving?

It's a bit hard to explain, but you must aspire to the sublime. The actual definition of the word *sublime* is noble. I have long believed, though, that it refers to our ability to sublimate our base human emotions, to rise above them. There surely is nobility to that. But here's my best shot at what the term means and where I think it comes from.

The word *con* in Latin means with; *fidos* in Latin means trust. *Con fidos* means with trust. It sounds a lot like confidence to me. Self-confidence means trusting in yourself. Once you really trust yourself you will be less focused on the relative game and more focused on your own journey, wherever it takes you. It's a true awakening.

No one has a perfect journey here on this planet. No one can escape without a degree of sadness (if you reach adulthood, chances are you will have had to attend a funeral of someone you loved) and so many other human emotions. But you must try not to defeat yourself. If you focus on others, chances are you will lose your way and start being guided by what you think others think. That is a total recipe for personal failure. That is why so many rich people end up so unhappy.

Mark Twain once said, "Courage is the mastery of fear, not the absence of fear." Want to get others to trust you? Trust in yourself. The way to trust in yourself is through practice. What kind of practice? Step back and acknowledge that you have doubts, that you are not all-powerful or all-knowing regardless of the photos in your office or the size of your paycheck. That's a good start.

During the great financial boom that preceded the great financial meltdown, very few market gurus had the self-confidence to step back and ask the hard questions of themselves and their companies: Can this growth be sustained? Are we doing things in the short term that will severely damage us in the long term? Is my paycheck a little too fat to be realistic? Morgan Stanley chief John Mack got paid $40 million in 2006, and then his firm came within days of failing as shareholders lost 80 percent of their money between July 2007 and late 2008. Richard Fuld, the head of Lehman Brothers, had several opportunities to sell his firm but couldn't get what he thought was a high enough price. On one Sunday night in September 2008, the firm simply turned off its lights and filed for bankruptcy, tossing thousands of people out of jobs and throwing the financial industry into an almost-fatal tailspin.

As evidenced by these stories, the Wall Street chiefs and seers who surrounded them exuded the belief that this time was different—that they understood the risks they were taking with other people's money and that it was all under control. From where did this hubris come? Most likely, it came from greed—the desire to make more money or to be immortalized in the annals of finance as the smartest or shrewd-est or toughest; to be seen as peerless.

These disgraced men all worked hard to achieve, but once atop the food chain, it seems they simply abandoned the habits that got them there. John Weinberg would have said they had swelled and not grown, at least not enough to understand how to manage the historically unprecedented situation around them and their roles in it. Computer models made people complacent. Money and the trappings of success made them overconfident and made them feel invincible.

Where they also failed was in not showing their weakness, not asking the hard questions surrounding their circumstances. It is a classic story; none of us is truly above it. We can throw eggs and tomatoes at Fuld or condemn John Thain because he spent over a million dollars on his office furniture. Yet these are smart guys. How could they go so wrong? And who among us in the same situation would have done better? Perhaps the money and the success light an uncontrollable fire.

■■■

There is a famous story in Homer's *Odyssey* where Odysseus tells the sailors to be wary of the mermaids, the sirens in the Mediterranean Sea. Their beauty and their songs will lure you into the rocks and to your eventual deaths. Wily Odysseus was afraid of this temptation and his accompanying weakness so he tied himself to the mast of the ship and blindfolded himself. The others? None of them took his advice and they were sucked into the sea and the treacherous whirlpool that the sirens tempted them toward. You have to know that this could be you. Or me. It isn't just the perceived Wall Street bad guys the media happens to be stick-whacking.

This story is as old as human history and the basis of most Greek tragedies. And just as with all parables, there is a moral to this story. In this case, it all boils down to knowing thyself. Ambition needs to be checked with a healthy dose of earthiness. When you are earthy, people can smell the dirt on you. When you are not, the force of gravity brought on by your hubris will eventually bring you down.

We watch these financial car crashes with hindsight and we judge them with the distance of bystanders on a high moral ground. Yet I submit that these people who caused these events are no different than any of us. In fact, without the right training and grounding, it is the usual outcome for human beings.

True self-confidence comes from the combination of discipline and the knowledge that you are prepared to answer the hard questions about yourself. It is not really all that daunting, and the difference might be just another hour a day of thought or exercise. It may mean reading or rereading the passages in Jim Collins' best seller *Good to Great* (HarperBusiness, 2001) on what it takes to be a Level 5 leader (hint: low-key, hard drive, compassion).

■ ■ ■

Richard Branson famously said: "I have been poor, now I am rich. Rich is better." Yeah, but he didn't say *he* was better, just that *it* was easier and more fun to be rich. Yet you get the sense that Branson probably had just as much fun when he was poor. He is adventurous, creative, and generally doesn't seem to care what people think about him. He's an example of how to live, rich or otherwise. He is ambitious, but what seems to drive him is something more compelling than money. It is a sense of being able to do what others can't or haven't tried. I have met Sir Richard several times and am always impressed with his earthiness and the fact that he recognizes that he is living a charmed life. There is a goofiness and a giddiness about him that resonates to the surface. He isn't spending much time trying to prove to you that he is the man. I don't really think he cares what others think, other than that he is a good man, living life to the fullest.

So, want a quick lesson on the road to the top?

- **Keep Your Ego in Check.** Although it is important to be confident, never let your self-assurance turn into arrogance; watch your ego. Confidence is part of the jet propulsion system that drives us to succeed, but the ego has to be handled carefully. A human brain high on money, prestige, success, and status can be like a dangerous hydrogen balloon (think *Hindenburg* here) unless it is grounded. And realize that luck and timing were probably involved in your success—you're not Superman.

It never ends well for the person who fails to keep a check on his ego. In his book *Happier: Learn the Secrets to Daily Joy and Lasting Fulfillment* (McGraw-Hill, 2007), Tal Ben-Shahar says that those who start each day from the perspective of appreciation and gratefulness are way happier than those who start the day thinking about all that has gone wrong in their lives. So start the day from a position of appreciation, but also ask yourself about the role of luck and timing in your life. Think about the many people who have helped you reach your goals and what the consequences would be if you were to lose it all. Think about your core values—do they conflict with the actions you are taking to make money?

- **Treat Everyone with Respect—Everyone.** I can still hear my grandmother telling me to treat everyone with respect and kindness. She worked in the school and was unafraid of hard labor. It is impossible for me not to see everyone as that woman who had the courage to leave her family and her country to come here to America, to work with her hands, and to try to make life better for her children and her grandchildren. It is a simple and humble act to show kindness. Keep it real.

  Part of treating others with respect is not judging others. You have to force yourself to put yourself in other people's shoes and learn about who they are before you judge them. If you are starting poor, you need to learn about rich people. If you are starting out rich, you need to learn about poor people. Don't just go with your bias. Don't begrudge a friend or colleague who has grown up rich, practices a certain religion, or adheres to certain cultural totems. Force yourself, expand your box of relationships, and slowly but surely you'll begin to recognize that we all are pretty much the same.

- **Try the Boy Scout Motto—Be Prepared.** If more Wall Street executives and subprime homebuyers had acted more like Boy Scouts than Gordon Gekko, perhaps there would have been a less calamitous economic outcome. You always need to be prepared and be on guard for all of the egomaniacs who are going to try to take advantage of you, as well as your own egotistical tendencies. Be practical, cautious, and careful. Give yourself periodic ambition assessments and then learn from your flaws so that you can make better choices.

It seems like the smartest among us haven't been able to escape some of the traps of ambition and ego, but let's learn from what happened and try to do better. Once again, we need to pull for each other and make it work.

Chapter 2

Success and Failure
Reaching for Excellence

I feel bad for you because none of you have ever failed at anything.
—*Ross Perot at Harvard Business School, 1987*

I was 13 years old and playing a night baseball game at the Police Athletic League field in Port Washington, the Long Island town where I grew up. We were behind. The opposing team had a 15-year-old pitcher and he had a great fastball. I was flailing at his pitches, weakly fouling them off. My ex-girlfriend, who had just ditched me for another guy, was up in the stands and rooting for the other team. Stomach butterflies, fear of failure, self-conscious anxiety, and adolescent jealousy were swirling in my head.

I was going to choke.

Then to my great surprise, with two strikes against me, I hit a ball into left centerfield that turned into a game-winning, inside-the-park home run. There is no way to describe the pure happiness of that moment.

So what's the big deal? It was just a Little League home run, right? Well, it was at that instant that it dawned on me: Don't fear doing. No matter the fears, rising up to meet challenges and swinging the bat is worth it. I have succeeded often: graduating Harvard Law School, working at Goldman Sachs, and then launching two very successful businesses. I've failed plenty—a couple of bar exams and a few jobs—but every time I think of doing something bold or audacious, I think of that hot summer night and my doubts begin to dissipate.

I'm smart enough to know that as easily as I hit a home run that night, I could've struck out, or popped up to the second baseman. I like to think I would've learned the same lesson—much like Ross Perot was trying to teach the B-school kids listening to his speech back in 1987.

Although I was in the law school at that time, I dropped by the talk because I was interested in hearing Perot speak. He was a fascinating guy, self-made, super-smart, and quirky enough not to be a cookie-cutter CEO. When I heard him speak, I was struck by that line about failure. I wasn't like a lot of the Harvard people. I wasn't bred for the Ivy League or following in anyone's footsteps. There's no Scaramucci Law Library on campus (yet) and I wasn't coming to the experience with perfect SAT scores, a prep-school pedigree, or any expectation that there wouldn't be bumps along the way. Heck, I'd already had them in high school and as an undergrad at Tufts. But here was old Ross, who five years later would begin his quixotic run for the White House, lecturing the failureless on failing. He was calling people out and they were bristling uncomfortably. But I sat there thinking: Yes, no way am I going to live a life of quiet desperation; I am going to push myself through the fear of failure.

■■■

There are always going to be potholes in life. You can't predict them, but failing is an important part of succeeding. Sometimes the truth is that simple. We grow by learning from our mistakes. These mistakes give us an ample number of teachable moments in our lives as long as we don't let them rattle our confidence.

In the United States, people are most fortunate as there are second acts. People can fail, dust themselves off, try again, and reinvent themselves. In many Western European countries it is too much of a loss of face and status to experience such failure, therefore there is less risk taking. Without such risk taking there isn't enough innovation or growth or success.

The culture of trying is truly American, yet many of us pick up the usual aristocratic fears, just the kind of thing Perot was describing. Why try and fail? There is too much pain in that, when instead you can go right up the middle and accept a life of mediocrity. These people can get very focused on the certainty of a destination, without really caring about the joy of the journey. This leads us to an identity crisis. Who are we? Are we exceptional or off track? This mind-set makes no sense to me.

Let's face it, failure sucks. We start out in la-la land, dreaming of a life where everything goes right and we fit it all in. No setbacks. Yet none of us lead the life we dreamed of growing up, not even those who you think do; secretly, they do not. They may just be better at hiding their imperfection.

Part of growth is failure and the adaptation and redirection that occur after it. This is the essence of what Perot was talking about that day. Don't be a wuss—if you have a dream, and especially if you live in the United States, you have a great chance to turn it into a reality.

My business school contemporaries listened to Perot, but whether it resonated with more than just me I honestly don't know. This question is now before all of us. Don't settle for mediocrity due to fear. Dare, dream, and do.

■■■

The yuppie puppies at Harvard, including me, all wanted to get down to Wall Street or start at a consulting firm. We signed up for the biggest, lowest-risk firms that we thought could offer the highest reward and paycheck. Goldman Sachs was the most effective of all the firms at recruiting the best and the brightest, and still is. Ace Greenberg, the legendary former boss of Bear Stearns (RIP), once said that he was recruiting "PSDs," those who are poor, smart, with a deep desire to be rich. Goldman recruited SCTs—the smartest, cleverest team players.

In 1989, I was hired as an associate in the investment banking division of Goldman Sachs—without having passed the bar. At Goldman Sachs, they surrounded you with a community. It was a great culture; there were smart people to hang out with and learn from and just about every major piece of support you could imagine, technical and otherwise. There were just a few rules: Play nice in the sandbox, don't openly try to kill each other. Collegiality. Passive Aggression. And say something that only another Goldman person could understand—speak in Goldmanspeak. For example:

Goldmanspeak: "John is not challenging himself enough."
Translation: "John is lazy."
Goldmanspeak: "Well, we are just going to have to agree to disagree."
Translation: "Are you kidding? I am a partner—fall in line or you're done."

And one of my all-time favorites:

Goldmanspeak: "I think we have a disconnect between what you think you are worth and what you actually are."
Translation: "We overpaid you. Time to shut up."

I was used to this Goldwellian dialogue. You know, no open fighting.

Goldman did so many things right and still does. They separated and empowered the bookkeepers and the lawyers and the traders and other moneymakers. Accountants and lawyers were respected and made partners, which made it way harder for prop traders to bully them. They waited before getting into new businesses, not wanting to be the early adopter but the group that enters the market after others have failed or had setbacks. They would copy the best parts and tweak and improve the worst parts of someone else's business plan. They taught and believed in ethics, had supertight compliance, and had what I called Goldman exceptionalism.

Goldman exceptionalism was the belief shared by many of its employees and others that the firm was better and more special than the others. This is a takeoff on American exceptionalism. It is something that magically makes people feel better about themselves and more purposeful.

A great place . . . too bad I got fired.

I failed.

One year and five months into my job at Goldman, I got fired. It was the scariest day of my life (at least up until that point). I was working in the real estate department at the time. I had joined the firm in August 1989 and absolutely bought into the conforming culture. I was assigned to help two vice presidents with deals. The job required a lot of spreadsheet work, stuff that I never did in college or law school. One of the vice presidents took me under his wing and tried to train and coach me; the other deemed me an imbecile and did her best to spread the word that "I just didn't get it." That was Goldwellian for "I was stupid and was never going to make it."

That was a death sentence at a place like Goldman. This wouldn't be good in a downturn, and first impressions for first-year associates don't change easily.

■■■

In late 1990, with the first Gulf War upon the nation and a weakened stock market, the real estate industry was suffering a sharp downturn. We had 100 people in the real estate investment banking department and there were going to be layoffs. The main person put in charge of doing these firings/conversations was Michael Fascitelli.

Mike, who is now the CEO of Vornado Realty Trust, was from Rhode Island, grew up in an Italian-American family, went to the University

of Rhode Island, and graduated from Harvard Business School. He
spent some time at the huge consulting firm, McKinsey, and then
joined Goldman in 1985. He was brilliant but was out of the ordi-
nary for Goldman as he had a huge, magnetic personality. Gifted with
numbers and people, he would eventually make partner in 1992, but
for now he was in charge of the strategic revamping of the real estate
department. He was working with the senior team to figure out who
were the keepers in the department. I wasn't a keeper.

I remember the day management was having the firing conversations.
When he came over to my desk I said, "Oh shit. Should I be putting up
a patriot missile defense? Is a Scud about to enter my cube?"

Again, it was the start of the Gulf War, and I was trying to be
funny. He laughed, a little. "Not yet, but if it happens I will be the one
to tell you."

I braced for impact.

Two days later his assistant called me and asked me if I could meet
Mike at his apartment on Jane Street. Not good. When I got there at
7 P.M. on February 1, 1991, I could feel the pit in my stomach. I had
passed over a few offers at some law firms to go to work at Goldman
(forever the right decision, by the way, no matter how my story ends)
and I was saddled with school debt.

He began, "Anthony, look, you are a great kid and because of our
personal relationship I could probably save you. But I am not going to."

After he gave me the severance speech, he said something I will
never forget. "I know I am doing the right thing for you. This job isn't
right for you and you've gotten off to a slow start. This whole thing
pains me—which is why I wanted to do it at my apartment. The right
thing for you is to get a job in sales and trading. I will do my best to try
to help you land something upstairs in Equities. You are going to have to
accept this and try to find your way into a job that better matches your
skill set."

I was angry but accepting. He absolutely did the right thing
and I respected him for it. But I was scared shitless. I needed some

source of cash and I was ashamed at getting tossed out of the first real job I'd ever had. I'd gone to Harvard Law School, for God's sake. It was my first job and a big failure—and at a place that I really wanted to be at and belong to. How could this be happening to me? But it was.

Of course, at that moment you want to blame anyone and everyone other than yourself. Part of it was my fault and part of it was because of the environment that we were in. But you know what? Mike was right: It was one of the best things that ever happened to me.

A cliché, but in my case, the absolute truth: The failure opened up a huge opportunity.

Two months later, with help from Mike, I landed a job in the firm's Equities Division and went into sales and eventually Private Wealth Management. I excelled at it. Michael and I are friends to this day, and I still rely on his mentorship and advice before making most major decisions in my life. When the vice president who gave me a hard time eventually left the firm, Mike interoffice-mailed me the name tag that adorned her office. The note said, "You are a tough bastard and outlasted your adversary." I laughed, but I have to tell you, the whole ordeal wasn't funny at the time. It forged a bond, though, between Mike and me. He was a guy you could trust to do the right thing even if the outlook in the short term looked bleak.

■■■

That brings me back around to my other big failure. It was late 1991 and I was thriving in the Equities unit at Goldman. I went to my boss and asked him if I could take two weeks off before the February 1992 bar exam.

He probed. "Why?"

I explained to him that while it wasn't something I needed for my job, it was a chapter in my life that I needed to close *and*, more importantly, I needed to know I could do it.

He said something very memorable: "Good for you. You need to be known as a finisher in life, not a quitter. I am glad that you are doing it."

A finisher. That's something I always want to be known as. I do not ever want to give up on something that is part of my goals. Finish. Never despair, even when you fall down. Do the ol' dust off and never, never ever quit—even if it means failing again.

Now, I am fully aware this is far easier in the abstract than it is to actually pull off. Pushing through failure, picking yourself up off the mat, moving that rubber tree plant, or any other old saw doesn't take into account the urgency of school loans, the needs or demands of family, and simply the ability to actually succeed at something. Sometimes, discretion can be the better part of valor. Walking away makes perfect sense. The key to life lies in knowing the difference between a fight that can't be won and a fight where you just need to gut out one more round before the tide turns.

That reality smacked me in the face, just about the time I decided I liked the idea of being a finisher. But I'm getting ahead of myself.

In July 1989, I had failed the bar exam. My grade was 656. Passing was 660. I missed it by one (*one!*) multiple choice question. Ouch. I had graduated from Harvard Law School, gotten a job at Goldman Sachs, and goosed the bar exam. Ouch. I had spent over $100,000 to get my Harvard Law School degree and started my career by failing the bar. Ouch. Was it a Camaro cruising relapse? I clearly let my guard down and blew it.

My parents still were upset that I wasn't going to be a lawyer. After all, hadn't I gone to law school? Try explaining to a mother and father, who didn't even have the chance to go to college, why a law school graduate doesn't become a lawyer:

"What do you mean you aren't going to practice law?"
"Don't worry, Mom, I will take the bar."

You can guess what happened. I didn't study enough. I didn't have my heart and soul in it. It was the summer after law school and I was out waterskiing and cavorting. I returned, briefly, to my high school ways. I was complacent.

I figured, "Hey how hard could it be? I only need a 66 to pass."

Congrats on the 65.6, dummy.

Now, I had good company in my failure. John F. Kennedy Jr. bombed the same exam. For me, I was embarrassed in front of my work friends and family. John Kennedy, however, had to fail publicly. "The Hunk Flunks" is what the *New York Post*'s headline screamed. It was painful.

I took the bar again in February 1990 and tried to study half-assed. Failed again. Guess what? John-John bit it again, too. The difference between us—minus the bloodlines and about seven inches of height— was that he was working for the Manhattan District Attorney and needed to pass, which he did the next July.

Not me. I was working at Goldman Sachs and was on several invest- ment banking assignments. I didn't need the bar for my job and I was too busy to try again. Yet failing that exam didn't help me professionally. It was foolish. That test was designed so that you could pass it, but you had to do the work. My bad.

I think my bar failure negatively affected my first impression to several bloodthirsty people at Goldman. If there is a moral of the story, it's this: You have to do everything in your power to make the first impression a fantastic one. Right clothes, right test scores, right swagger. I was still a touch immature, and I bought it and lost when I shouldn't have.

This thought also didn't escape me: Failing the bar was embarrass- ing, nettlesome, and unnecessary, but it was certainly easier than failing at something I truly loved and wanted. I wasn't a writer who'd spent his life working at a part-time job to allow myself time to craft an epic novel, only to have it turned away in favor of *Chicken Soup for the Soul*. Had I wanted to be a lawyer, had I grown up watching *Perry Mason* and fantasizing about courtrooms and closing arguments, my bar brawl might have been soul-crushing.

The failure hurt, though, and I can remember telling people about it and seeing some shock on their faces. It was from a combination of disbelief that I failed it but also that I was stupid enough to talk about it and share the experience with others. That was bad personal advertising. Dude, if you failed, keep your mouth shut. But I was 25 and vulnerable. I'm confident that several of my colleagues thought it was equally dumb to share my experience about the failure, but I didn't see it that way. I failed. It sucks, but I was determined not to make it the be-all and end-all.

I often think about some of the people who looked at me funny, and I think, "That's too bad that you are so worked up about failure and the perception of it." Those people are like, "Wow, that's terrible, and it better never happen to me." That's too bad, because we all need a little bit of failure so we can learn to stretch ourselves.

And so it wasn't until February 1992 that I took the exam and passed. I took two weeks off from Goldman Sachs before that exam and studied 14 hours a day. In November that year I was admitted to the bar. Bottom line: I had finished what I started. It mattered to me and it was another wake-up call.

My failure had now become a success.

■ ■ ■

One major problem with success is that as it builds up, you want to keep adding to it, and you can sometimes become fearful of trying new things. We think, "It feels good to succeed, so why stretch and do something stupid that casts me in a bad light?"

That is the prevailing thought that Perot urged those Harvard kids to break away from. Essentially, the point of Perot's speech was to not be afraid to make another choice. There is joy in originality. In their lives, they had tested well from as far back as their Montessori days, been valedictorians of their high school class, and progressed nicely within the pack of achievers into which they had been assimilated.

This is not to say they weren't smart or didn't work harder than most; their success up to a point in their lives, however, had become a reflex more than a passion.

So for the Harvard, Wharton, Stanford crew, failing represented something alien. Imagine leaving B-school to start a gourmet shop, or leaving Goldman to become a high school teacher. The risk of failure is even greater then, because you have removed yourself from a familiar track and opted for another one. How do you get back on? Will you ever catch up? Does failing at something make it impossible for you to ever do anything worthwhile again?

These sorts of questions paralyze people and keep them on a steady career track to maintain relative income and social status. This permanent-success pattern can sometimes create an unruly Wall Street CEO who has never tasted defeat or experienced any real hiccups, and somehow thinks failure is unimaginable. This is a recipe for uber-arrogance and the big failure, the one that is never, ever expected. The unsinkable ship, the *Titanic*. The unsinkable firm, Lehman Brothers.

Failure can happen to any of us. It all depends on the path and the relative success that we attain. It's easy in school. We all take the same test, study the same things, and attend the same job fairs. We balance things out and measure them relatively. But once we've done everything expected and still feel empty, we're puzzled about the next move. I think the emptiness comes from the pursuit of things that we think are necessary in order to be perceived by our peers as successful. The picture-perfect life, the right job, right title, right salary, right place to live . . . all of the stuff that *Men's Health, GQ,* and *Cosmo* tell us we need to be. Yet think about how often the ones that grace the covers of these magazines are those who have dared to take a risk, to be a little different and a lot unique.

When we decide that our next move is toward something we've always wanted but maybe never figured out how to pursue or never had the guts to chase, we get scared.

What holds us back? Many times, it's more than the fear of failure—it is the perceived consequential *embarrassment* of failing, or the fear of being different from our peers. At 20, we care deeply what other people think about us; at 40 we realize they were only thinking about themselves; and at 60—well, we realize that it doesn't really matter what others think. (Okay, so I am not 60 yet, but many of my trusted friends and mentors have handed this wisdom down to me.) It's natural to care what others think; we just need to be careful that we don't make it our consuming passion. We can get a lot wrong by worrying about others.

The first step toward moving away from this sort of thinking is to work at erasing our personal insecurities and building our self-confidence. Self-confidence is habit-based—a quiet belief and enough humility to realize no man is isolated, whether he succeeds or fails. There is a family around him, a community in which he lives, and a culture that somehow rewards his achievements and buffers his falls. The ability to encourage oneself and exude a sense of purpose cannot be discounted—living without the fear of failure, and also living without the fear of success.

One good way to build up our self-confidence and get over the fear of failure and insecurities we're all born with: public speaking.

I do a lot of public speaking and television appearances. I realize that even in today's overly media-oriented society, that's rare. Most people fear public speaking more than they fear death. There is something about our brains that makes us feel uncomfortable when people are staring at us; then the self-conscious genes kick in and we get freaked out. We start to think: "Am I saying or doing something that is going to lead to permanent, lifelong embarrassment?"

Know this, there are really very few things that can take you out of the game. At the 1988 Democratic Convention, Arkansas Governor Bill Clinton was given the opportunity to speak, and he spoke for so long and was so boring that when he said, "And so in conclusion . . ." the conventioneers cheered. It set him back, but I don't think it really hurt his career. Short of spewing racist invective or inciting people to kill the president, there's nothing you can say that can't be corrected or apologized for.

On the flip side, doing even a little public speaking earns the respect of those around you, especially if you do it well. It also helps you reach the goal of not caring what others think of you. Sure, someone in the audience can criticize or heckle, but they wouldn't be willing to trade places with you. That's the kind of quiet courage that goes a long way.

Public speaking can be learned. It requires practice, but here are three simple tips that have been paraphrased from Franklin Roosevelt:

1. Keep it short.
2. Be sincere.
3. Sit down.

I would add just one more: Be intimate with the audience and imagine you're talking to just one person. That way everyone in the audience will think the person is them and they will be forced to listen.

Warren Buffett often talks about taking a Dale Carnegie public speaking course in his youth. I did the same thing in April 1989 with my college roommate (and future presidential aide) Rick Lerner. We learned how to stand, how to deal with the butterflies, the uhs, and the ums. We also learned that everyone—and I mean everyone—has at least a little fear of public speaking.

The Dale Carnegie course was fantastic for forcing practice. Get up in front of people as much and as often as you can. Be brief, though—always leave an audience wanting more. Try doing it without a teleprompter or reading from excessive notes; this will keep people off of their BlackBerrys while you are talking. And remember, over time you can inoculate yourself from the paralyzing sort of fear, but we all start out with some of it, and we need to overcome it if we want to be successful.

■ ■ ■

The second step in getting rid of the fear of failure is to avail yourself to the better parts of your personality and don't let the fear wash over everything you are. Sometimes we peek our heads out like little prairie dogs and we get stomped. It is at that moment that we have to decide who we are going to be. It's easy to cower, take a back seat, and let embarrassment take over: "I can't do this, can't be this. I am too short, not smart enough, too fat."

Luckily, there is a better way. You know those days when you feel like you can conquer the world? You know what? On those days, you're still not tall enough and still a few IQ points short of Einstein. And it doesn't matter. It actually *never* matters. What matters is that you pursue what satisfies you—what you want to define you. When you do that, you become blind to your shortcomings because you are occupied with a goal that's bigger.

Failure of the dramatic kind should be an interviewing prerequisite on Wall Street. Too often it's the cookie-cutter perfect person who gets the job. I think it would be an interesting suggestion for the Wall Street recruiting departments (and other professions) to throw in the failure interview question. "Ever fail at anything? What was your worst moment and how did you rebound?" It might make for a better class of traders and bankers if they searched for those who have bounced back a little. No bouncing could indicate that an unexpected fall will lead to a breakdown.

For Wall Street, the events of 2008 were pretty humbling, yet I am sure there are many Masters of the Universe out there who are unbowed because they do not know how to balance success with failure. No matter—you need to push yourself into areas that you want to go into, despite your fears and any social stigma. The setbacks can shave the edges of arrogance and overconfidence off of most personalities. They can also add resilience and reduce long-term fears. Hopefully failure will put you closer to your ultimate success. And it adds sweetness, kindness, for failure is humbling. It doesn't, however, have to be defeating.

Force yourself to think like that a little every day. Ignore the bad and focus on the strong points. Remember, on the days you fail, you're still good at things, loved by your kids and dog, whatever. Failure is isolated, not all-encompassing.

And for the new graduates or recently unemployed out there who are still looking for a job, don't let the failure to find one thus far pull you down. There is something like 38 percent unemployment among the recent college graduating classes. While you can't use that as an excuse, you have to realize that you are searching for a job in a historically hard economic environment. Chin up. Learn from the setback and the unplanned unemployment. Grow. Take a risk.

■ ■ ■

I also think that those who lose their fear of failing no longer fear dissent. The more open people can be with you, the stronger you can become. Those who fear failure—or have never failed—often seek out yes-men and yes-women. (We'll get to examples of these Gekko-like sheep in a few minutes.) They want to be praised and never want to be questioned. Now of course it's a lot of fun to have people fawning over you and it can make you feel all-powerful, but the truth is it won't help to make you stronger or more successful. In fact, it will reinforce certain weaknesses. If people can't call you out or explain your weaknesses, how can you expect to get better?

Essentially, failing is a great opportunity for honest self-assessment. Then again, succeeding should be, too. In both cases, there's a combination of skill, hard work, and luck. We are just more likely to publicly attribute our successes to the first two and our failures to a lack of the third.

Let's flash back to Wall Street and the meltdown. In fact, let's specifically look at Lehman Brothers. In 2003, I found myself as an employee of Lehman. How did that happen? In 2001, we sold Oscar Capital— the hedge fund and wealth management company that I started with Andrew K. Boszhardt Jr. when I left Goldman—to money management giant Neuberger Berman. In 2003, Lehman Brothers bought Neuberger. (I'll get to this story later in the book.)

By late 2004 it was clear to me that the senior executives at Neuberger Berman were going to be departing, and Lehman wanted to populate the management team with a group of guys who bled team-green.

Lehman had a group at the top who were tightly knit. They had the following characteristics: Each of them had spent 20-plus years at the firm, worked closely with Chairman Dick Fuld—or his right-hand man, Joe Gregory—and were loyal to the firm and to each other. It was particularly hard for an outsider to break in. The firm had an immuno-defense system that would set off an intruder alert if you were a lateral hire.

In some ways this made sense. These guys were protective of each other and the franchise. They had a lottery ticket, punched years ago, that gave them access to millions of dollars a year in compensation. They had lived together through ups and downs.

Sometimes having that kind of tribal nature can help a firm as it makes people feel purposeful. In the case of Lehman, however, a lot of what killed the firm came from that very culture. Without a critical-thinking process and challenge of the status quo, things die. All great organizations and political systems need checks and balances. Without them, complacency and groupthink sets in. Our founding fathers, specifically Hamilton, wrote about this in the Federalist Papers. Buy the Cliff Notes if necessary, but read about it.

Essentially, ambitious people want (and need) to be intellectually challenged. At Lehman, these challenges were blunted and almost treated as if they were treason. Express a point of view different from the regime, and you were on the outs. This led to a culture of yes-men and yessing. The people inside senior management wanted things to stay the same, but what makes life so interesting is that they don't.

As you can imagine, it was very hard to challenge people in an environment that didn't like change. Lehman had survived a near-death experience in 1998, when the Long-Term Capital Management failure and the Russian currency collapse sent the global economy into a tailspin. That it had survived against long odds made management think their success was more skill and hard work than luck. Perhaps it was, but one thing it did was reinforce their belief that they would always find a way out of the rubble. They had great confidence in their ability to overcome any crisis.

Yet Lehman also had Goldman Sachs envy: "We are just as good as Goldman. We are on track to be like them, to be as profitable, as good." I can guarantee you, no one at Goldman was saying that they were just as good as Lehman.

Think of it this way: When you are the Kansas City Royals you have to realize you are the Kansas City Royals, and even though you want to be the New York Yankees, you live in Kansas City and have to deal with the exigencies of the smaller market as it relates to talent and opportunity. Lehman guys wanted to be the New York Yankees, which was something that they weren't. I used to laugh about how excited they got when they hired former Goldman people. Senior people, not junior Goldman people like I was. They would immediately put those guys on a pedestal; it was the only time the intruder alert and the immune-defense went dark. I worked for both, so I can tell you that the difference is that Goldman managers were smart enough and secure enough to bring people in to challenge their thought process, retest their theories, and encourage productive dissent.

Endemic to this thought process and envy was that the Lehman managers were losing their ability to adapt. Alternative viewpoints, if we are strong and confident enough to hear them, help us to adapt and improve our thought process. We hear something different from our own opinion and it makes us rethink our views, maybe refine them and make them better. Yet Lehman was a culture that frankly couldn't do that. In fact, it was the opposite.

There is a difference between treason and honesty with a thought to make things better. This is one of the reasons I get along so well with Oliver Stone, the director of *Wall Street* and *Money Never Sleeps*. While we may not match up on many political views, I enjoy hearing his opinions and, more importantly, hearing his reasoning. He loves the country, he just doesn't buy into the establishment. Having him on the team makes the whole better. Oliver also believes in dissent, and I think he enjoys riling up the establishment. You need to hear dissent to test and refine your theories, make them better.

There were no Oliver Stones at Lehman. Poke at something there and you were gone. For instance, Mike Gelband, the head of fixed income, thought they were taking on too much unknowable risk. Bye-bye Mike Gelband. Not good. He returned at the suggestion of Bart McDade, but it was too late. The iceberg was hit; now only deck chairs could be rearranged.

Adapt or die. We all fight that battle. In Lehman's case, the inability to confront failure and adapt to change added more and more risk to the firm. People who were trusted weren't checked aggressively. There was none of the Reagan-era "trust but verify" discipline. The lack of it imperiled the entire firm.

Then when the great meltdown started, the firm was caught unaware. Regulators had been warning it for months, and management had several opportunities to sell to larger firms but, convinced of their enormous worth, rejected them. By the last weekend of its life, Lehman's top dogs were working hard and skillfully trying to make a deal. Then they ran out of luck when the government decided it wasn't worth being rescued. A bum deal? Maybe. But was it a failure that could have been avoided with some critical self-assessment? Without a doubt.

I also think that the failure was a result of Lehman's senior management upsetting the Feds (Paulson, Geither, et al.). As we saw in Chapter 1, this is classic hubris. The political environment was such that someone needed to be made an example of—and they chose to make an example out of Lehman. Let me ask you, if you need to make an example of someone, are you going to put down a friend or take a group that hasn't exactly endeared itself to you? It is sort of obvious. Yet I am sure to this day the vanquished are still incredulous. And the government officials will hide behind their "lack of legal authority" argument, meaning they will say that they had no legal options in front of them to bail out Lehman. I think it is a poor alibi. They were waving wads of money at things and could have gotten post hoc authority for any decision because of the heat of the crisis.

Wishful thinking without self awareness and checks and balances leads to the wrong type of tombstones. In September 2008, Lehman's was inscribed with RIP.

Now, I am not saying that I could have done better than they did. All I am saying is that we should examine their failure and dedicate ourselves to the proposition of learning from it and seeing if we can apply it to our own companies, businesses, careers, or even personal lives.

I personally felt Lehman should have been saved since they had made the decision to do some saving. Do it all rather than being in the middle. The government, unless you're talking about World War II, likes going halfway: Vietnam, Afghanistan, Iraq (before the surge), and the Wall Street meltdown (before the collapse of Lehman). Half measures. To the government's credit, once Lehman failed they got scared and provided ample backstop. For a decade the Japanese have tried lots of half measures, and what did they get? A lost decade. In March 2009, Fed Chairman Bernanke gave his "we'll helicopter money; no one else is going to fail" speech and we have been on a stock market tear ever since. Markets and people like confidence, Bernanke and the government supplied it, and the crisis for now has abated, though it tore a deep wound into the real economy.

So would stick-to-itiveness and no-men have saved Lehman? I am all for tenacity, but you have to assess where you are and where you are going, not just where you *want* to be going. We always need to be realistic. While tenacity is an important ingredient in the mix that leads to success, it can bring ruin without self-awareness.

In the case of Lehman, it was the wrong kind of tenacity. They needed to adjust and to change course; they needed to challenge the status quo. Tenacity saved them in 1998, but the waves were too high in 2008. One of the problems Lehman had was that many of the people running the firm had never worked on their own, made a payroll on their own, or had any sense of dramatic personal failure. As a result, they had blinding self-arrogance and a lack of understanding of what could really go wrong. When it happened, they were shocked. Today I am sure they still are.

Warren Buffett believes the reason we have such poor corporate governance is because of polite incompetence where it's rude for corporate board members to disagree with management and each other. He believes that better corporate governance requires dissent. The consensus isn't cutting it. The silence is deafening in these sorts of situations. It's your life—speak up. Or as Mel Gibson said when he portrayed William Wallace in *Braveheart*, "Every man dies; not every man really lives." Think about one life, one voice; be yourself, don't co-opt.

■ ■ ■

I wonder if the colossal collapse in our economy will be burned into a generation of people, or if it will be just a blip on their radar? Will this failure ultimately help us succeed in the future? The problem with global meltdowns is that they can absolve a lot of individual guilt. You can sweep a lot of personal shortcomings under the rug of the crisis by saying, "Don't blame me, blame the crisis." Personalizing things is often a bad idea, but I hope that whatever you experienced during that time and its aftermath prepared you for the future. We do some of our best learning when we are being crushed and have failed. We learn the most about our character when we spring back.

Barack Obama and Bob the Builder share the mantra of "Yes, we can." I encourage people to say "I can do this" to themselves every day, quietly and out loud. These are four magical words. Say it often and believe it so that when you suffer a setback you can step back, catch your breath, and resume the pursuit of your goals. You need to suffer setbacks; otherwise, you are not truly pushing yourself. Without feeling that self-conscious pain and concomitant anxiety, you will never develop the right empathy for others or worldly experience.

To this point, it is important, especially for young people, to seek out the right sort of mentors. Challenge yourself to be the best version that you can be. Define it, and then believe it. You will do yourself a great service if you fall back into the arms of your own journey. Try to relax and trust in your own destiny.

Dreaming, planning, and executing goals with courage and without fear are all ingredients for success. Being humble and recognizing that all of these roads to self-actualization, some leading to temporary setbacks and momentary failures, are part and parcel of finding your fortune without losing your soul. All of this is hard work. Ever look at somebody who has looks, brains, and talent, yet doesn't seem to be going anywhere? Chances are they haven't put in the work, haven't developed the self-confidence and combined it with discipline and perseverance. They probably had a few bad breaks and it is likely that they gave up in fear of failing again. Who knows? I will never pretend to know what is going on in the life of someone else. However, if you don't peel yourself off the canvas after you have been knocked down, you just lost the opportunity to reach your goals. Don't let it happen to you.

It is not really all that daunting. The difference might be just another hour a day of thought and practice—an hour less on Facebook, or on the couch flipping through 200 cable channels, or playing *Call of Duty*. One thing's for sure, when you work hard to accomplish a task and good things happen, it breeds on itself. In the book *Outliers: The Story of Success* (Little Brown and Company, 2008), Malcolm Gladwell credits practice as one of the biggest factors in deriving success. Practice like crazy. Do it with enthusiasm.

Perhaps the crisis has set us up for another renewal. I hope so, but if not, make sure that you're ready. Think about what you need to do today to create a better tomorrow for yourself. Push. We can do better—yes we can.

■ ■ ■

I have had several meaningful failures that I am sometimes put off by, still painful to this day. The pain carves experience into the brain and provides hard-to-forget lessons. I would argue that without failure you can't really progress to whom and what your ultimate essence is. If I hadn't failed during my early days at Goldman, I might have struggled along as a middling investment banker. Instead, it made me realize what I bring to the table. I suspect that I knew it all along but needed a lesson from the outside world to bring it to my awareness. But that was a tough sell in the week after being dumped. Failure is a cold-water awakening. You suck—now what? What are you made of?

There are three simple rules for dealing with failing and turning it into success:

1. **Admit It.** Don't be embarrassed by it. I can remember being out to dinner with one of my Goldman colleagues and his wife, when he blurted out, "Well, at least I never failed at anything like Anthony." They were having an argument at the dinner table and he turned to her and said that. A quiet dinner at a suburban restaurant on Long Island turned into a seminal moment. Okay, back then I was pissed when I heard it. Upon reflection I am laughing. This was a guy who was going to cookie-cutter his way through life and his career, never once putting his ego in harm's way or taking a risk. Yikes. To really succeed, and find your fortune, you have to be bigger than that. Take the risks, admit when you mess up, and deal with the pain. Adjust and adapt.

2. **Set Yourself up for Success.** Success is hard work, audacity, grit, and courage. It is also about delaying gratification. You have to be willing to be the ant. Remember, the grasshopper gets the shaft in the end. Associate with people who feel the same way.

    Plan. Flow. Adapt. Plan. Flow. Compromise. Adapt. Plan—all the while trying to execute and strive for success. I started in the Goldman Sachs Real Estate Corporate Finance Department 20 years ago. Now I am a managing partner of a global hedge fund seeding business. Along the way, I've owned an ice cream parlor that failed (I refer to that as the First Great Meltdown) and have launched and sold another hedge fund/money management business. Be prepared for the twists and turns, and it will turn out that you can still be a success, even if it isn't success the way you defined it on your post-graduation goals list. It will be unique, though, and rewarding, particularly if you worked hard to earn it.

And, remember, there will be missteps along the way. Be flexible, we all have to brace for the impact of the unexpected.

3. **When Rough Road Appears, You Must Face Your Worst Fears.** Will I reach my goals? Fulfill my dreams? What is my destiny and how well will I deal with it? Some failures are speed bumps; others are craters. Of course, all of us want to avert failure, yet to achieve and fulfill dreams we need to accept it, and overcome it. And sometimes we have to accept that certain things are just not going to happen for us. No, if you are recently graduating from Harvard Law School, you are not going to be the Chief Justice of the Supreme Court, a self-made billionaire, *and* President of the United States. Sounds like fun, but it takes a few lifetimes for all of that. The important thing is to be patient, practice, and take chances.

Follow this advice, and failure becomes a temporary setback for you. Follow it well, and you'll have empathy to support and lift others.

Chapter 3

Vocation and Meaning
Let It All Hang Out

People who have money don't need people.

—*Alex P. Keaton*

Alex P. Keaton was just a character on the hit 1980s TV show *Family Ties*. Played expertly by the awarding-winning Michael J. Fox, he was the arch-conservative, avaricious teenage son of liberal parents who idolized Ronald Reagan, promoted supply-side economics, and always carried around a leather briefcase. He wanted to grow up and become a mogul, an entrepreneurial wunderkind. What he didn't have was a moral compass. Big comedic lines in the show were about his lack of sensitivity and bottom-line orientation.

In a lot of ways, Alex P. Keaton symbolized my generation. We came of age with Ronald Reagan, young enough to find ideals but jaded enough by the failures of the Carter administration that we became more Drexel Burnham than Peace Corps. Yup, Alex P. Keaton, the love child of Ayn Rand and Gordon Gekko, was a guy we'd all actually hang out with. And the Alex P. Keatons around me in the 1980s wanted to make money—lots of it.

What did I want to do when I grew up? Although I wasn't entirely sure, I too wanted to make money. In March 1984, the law firm of Cravath, Swaine & Moore was paying first-year associates a starting salary of $65,000 a year. That, my friends, was a lot of dough. I thought that was all the money I could ever want or need. After all, my folks probably raised my brother, sister, and me on less. With these dollar signs—I mean, thoughts—in mind, I decided then and there that I would go to law school. Specifically, I geared myself toward becoming a Wall Street lawyer. Don't ask me if I really knew what that meant. I knew guys on Wall Street made a lot of money and I knew lawyers made a lot of money. I imagined the two combined. Who could want more than that?

I took the LSAT and applied to seven schools, got into six (Yale, of course, didn't see the value of having me on campus). On February 6, 1986—Ronald Reagan's 75th birthday, if you're keeping score at home— Harvard Law School accepted me. Perfect. It was only two miles from Tufts, I loved Boston, and it was *Harvard*. I was thrilled. I had finally detoxed from my mediocre high school career and, through hard work and dedication, fulfilled the promise I had made to Sol Gittleman to reach for my full academic potential. Four weeks before I got accepted, one of my buddies at school came over to me, put his arm around me, and said: "Hey, I heard from Harvard Law School today, and I got in. Did you?"

"What, me?" I replied. "Uh, no, I haven't heard yet."

"Really? I thought you and I put our applications in at the same time."

Well you can't imagine the pain and anxiety of the conversation for me. At 22, it meant so much to me and I really wanted it. Looking back, I realize that I am fortunate that it went my way, but I am also wise enough to know I would've been just fine if it hadn't.

In any case, I was going to law school and I knew with absolute certainty that I was going to be a Wall Street lawyer. (Yet, as you know from reading this book, it never happened—how ironic). I still laugh at that. I had ingrained in my brain my future simply because of its accompanying salary.

Before my first year, I headed straight for the law school's admissions office, paid my deposit, and got a copy of both the alumni directory and the recruiting directory, which had contact information for all the major law firms. I typed up my resume on a Panasonic typewriter and headed for Wall Street.

It sounds moronic now, but my first stop was One Wall Street because, well, it was the first one listed. I thought Wall Street lawyers actually worked on Wall Street. At that time, the beautiful art deco building was called the Irving Trust Building, and on its 28th floor the venerable law firm of Hughes Hubbard & Reed had its main lobby. Don't know them? Well, at the turn of the last century, Charles Evan Hughes was a presidential candidate and he eventually became a Supreme Court Justice. The firm was located at One Wall Street and it *was* a law firm, so I had to try to get a summer job. I took the elevator to the main floor and asked the receptionist if I could meet with one of the partners whose name I had circled in the Harvard Law School alumni directory.

"Is this a cold call?" she asked. "We don't allow solicitations here."

"No, I am going to Harvard Law School next year," I said proudly, "and I was hoping he would speak to me. Can you please tell him I'm here?"

Sure enough, he came out and brought me down to his beautiful corner office.

I began my pitch: "Sir, I would like a summer job. I am willing to do anything and I know that I can be a productive member of your team. I start at Harvard Law School in the fall and need to make some money to afford the tuition. Would you please help me?"

He looked at me. "Okay. We'll give you a summer job as a paralegal and start you at $8 per hour."

That selfless move prompted a response that only could've been channeled from my Uncle Sal (you'll hear about him later—at the time, he was the craftiest businessman I'd ever met): "Could you make it $10?"

"What?"

I repeated: "Could you make it $10? I really could use the money."

And so $10 it was.

And I worked for every penny of it, morning to midnight—for 60 straight days.

That summer, the economy was booming and we were working on the People's Express/Continental Airlines merger. The deal, from what I could make out, was big and important; the people at the firm were nice; but the job was boring and repetitive. I felt like I was in the Dickens novel *Bleak House*, on a mind-numbing and soul-killing journey along a trail of contracts, sale leasebacks, and loan agreements. It was a summer job that spanned 60 days and it felt like six years. I felt stifled. And even though I was supposed to be loving my life as an up-and-coming law school student, I was just a suburban rube in the big city. From what I could tell, the 29-year-old fourth-year associate basically had the same job as me. Sure, he got paid more, but we were more or less doing the same thing, and whatever that was certainly wasn't enough for me—I didn't have the passion for it. But try telling your parents you're having second thoughts about attending law school a few weeks before your first day!

I started Harvard Law School in September, deeply committed . . . to not end up a lawyer.

■ ■ ■

It is often said that those who convert are the most strident believers. That was certainly the case for me, and it was clear that I needed to find a job outside of law. My search became an obsession. The more obsessed I was, the more driven I became.

I found the escape hatch from this career during my third year of law school (I know, I know, I could've moved faster). I went to a recruiting day Goldman Sachs was holding at the Charles Hotel in Boston. To this day, I remember the name of the Goldman executive who was there: Suzanne Nora Johnson. Before going to Goldman, Suzanne had attended Harvard Law School and then worked as an attorney for Simpson Thacher & Bartlett. One of the most talented people at Goldman, she eventually became a partner and rose to head of research before she retired a few years ago. These days she's on the board of Intuit and the Brookings Institute. In 2009, I had the pleasure of participating with her on a luncheon panel at the World Economic Forum in Davos, Switzerland. But back in 1988, we hit it off instantly and she invited me down to New York for a second round of interviews.

Around the same time, I was interviewing at other financial firms. Right after I received a rejection letter from Shearson Lehman Hutton, who castigated me for not reading *Barron's* or the *Wall Street Journal*, I started reading them and the *New York Times* business section. For my Goldman interview, I read a fascinating article in *Institutional Investor's* January 1984 edition titled "Inside the Goldman Sachs Culture." It talked about group cooperation and creating a one-firm culture. I devoured the article and memorized the names of the central players. I didn't know how to do a macro on a Lotus spreadsheet, but I did know a lot about the firm and what made it special. In my mind, I was prepared for my Goldman interview more than anything else in my life. And, like the Alex P. Keatons around me, I really wanted to work there.

My second big break after meeting Suzanne was interviewing with Robin Josephs and Frank Walter for a job in real estate finance at Goldman. Robin was a rising star inside the firm. She was beautiful, smart, and sincere. In 1986, the firm had made Jeannette Loeb its first woman partner, and there was a feeling in the air that being a woman was no longer awkward and stifling for a career on Wall Street. Frank had worked for Kenneth D. Brody, the head of the department, and had come to the firm from the military. He was incredibly well liked and was one of the early favorites in his class to be a partner.

Although it wasn't easy for me to get a job at a place like Goldman, Robin took a liking to me for some reason. "You're different from who we usually hire," she said in a way that had me confused. How different? Well for starters I had no experience in corporate finance. I was 24 and had no real idea what they did. What I knew, however, was that I didn't want to be a lawyer.

But I was talking too much, still one of my problems today. I even followed one partner, Bill Gruver, who was interviewing me, into the bathroom to finish my enthusiastic thought. Not good. I had to be coached by a few people who wanted to hire me to shut up. Well, at least I was coachable.

Frank Walter and Robin Josephs called me one afternoon and said that they were willing to go to the next round with me, but they wanted me to do a little work. They sent me some material related to the dividend discount model and how to derive a net present value on a Hewlett Packard calculator known as an HP12c.

During our next interview, Frank said, "Anthony, there is something about you that I think the firm needs. Your answers aren't stock, like something out of the Harvard Business School employee placement handbook. You are original and authentic. The truth is you will be an experiment here. But we all like you." They took a chance on me and I am forever grateful.

In December 1988, I accepted the job with a start date of August 1989. Frank Walter announced that he was leaving the firm in February 1989. Although I hadn't known Frank very long, I was shocked and disappointed—I didn't understand why he would leave an established, brand-name firm that paid him a high salary. He explained to me that he made the decision to leave the firm so he could spend more time with his wife and family. There was a saying at Goldman that "Your family is first, but Goldman is a close second." Frank's actions made it clear that the saying was Goldmanspeak. The motto should have been: "We devour all of your time." The divorce rates inside the firm were high and Frank didn't want to be another statistic. Soon after he left, he joined forces with some retired Goldman partners and built a real estate investment business. He is still a close friend and the kind of guy with whom you would trust your savings and your children. He would have been a partner there, yet he walked away from it. Something that means so much to so many didn't mean enough to Frank. Goldman über alles? Not for him. Unlike the young, naïve, and somewhat greedy Alex P. Keatons of my generation, he had found his moral compass, vocation, and meaning in life. He chose his real family, just as I was about to join my second one.

■ ■ ■

I was not the pick of the litter in my investment banking training class. As you found out in Chapter 2, I didn't exactly knock the cover off the ball in my first job. In the midst of a mass layoff in 1991, Goldman sent me packing. Thanks to Mike Fascitelli, I got a second chance at the firm and found my spot in sales in the firm's Equities Division. In 1994, I moved into the Private Client Services group. We were 100 brokers who served some of the world's wealthiest people, many of whom made millions going public with Goldman as their bankers.

From a cultural perspective I was actually doomed at Goldman. Forever I would be known as a banker who had failed, so I was transferred into a different area—the land of the private bankers. One time, after a heated discussion with my boss about bonuses, he reminded me I had little to complain about. "After all, we fired you from banking—you are lucky that you are here." I was immature and probably whining at the time, and he took out the 12-gauge Goldman language shotgun. With more maturity I would probably have been less sore and sensitive to remarks like that, but they stung and altered my behavior.

A lesson for all the young people reading this book: It's a job. Don't allow what is said to you to be taken too personally. If you let your detractors get inside your melon, then you will ultimately lose your soul, self-confidence, and individuality. Be wary: Melons are soft, and sharp knives can cut right through. People inside large and small companies each have their own unique agendas. Some are actually diabolical and Machiavellian. So you need to learn how to play the game, put your emotions aside, swallow your pride, and focus on enhancing your skill set—and if that doesn't work, you'll need to start your own company.

Remember, the best version of you is the way you define yourself when you are daydreaming. There is also a worst version of you, and if you hang out with the wrong people, guess what? The worst version floats to the top. Being told that I was a failed banker often and regrettably brought out the worst version of me. I was overly self-conscious about this perception. I needed to relax a little. I was in the right spot and doing well but I couldn't shake the perceived stigma. Melon-head me was split right open. So sensitive and insecure was I that I was angry and anxious when I should have been confident and relaxed.

Over time, though, I became more at ease and consequently more confident in my role in the company. Private banking at Goldman Sachs was originally called Securities Sales. No fancy name back then, and after all, what did we do? We sold securities to individuals—we were glorified retail brokers. I was given a desk and a phone, a few business cards, and months of training. The firm would foot expenses and a base salary, which ultimately became a draw against commissions once you broke through and made enough to be on commission. It took me 11 months to get there. That was an absolutely painful process. I had never seen the inside of a country club and I had no family contacts that could possibly meet the $5 million minimum needed to open up a Goldman Sachs retail account. It was countless calls, meetings with accountants and lawyers, perusing IPO prospectuses, and in general, me on my knees begging.

By the eighth month I was still bone-dry and hadn't opened up one account. I went to see Todd Morgan, one of the partners in charge of the division who is now the CEO of a company called Bel Air Investment Advisors.

"Todd, I have tried everything and I can't open an account. I am anxious that I am going to get fired again. Tell me, what should I do?"

"Well, the good news for you, Anthony, is that you are right on schedule. I am surprised that the rest of your class isn't lined up at my door behind your sorry ass."

He then went on to explain that no one in my group had yet opened a substantial account—and that was okay, since there was a sales process that took at least 9 to 12 months. He said, "Around that point, there would be a change in circumstance—someone would sell their business and remember the meeting that they had with you and give you a call." You were at Goldman Sachs, after all. It had a fabulous brand name and people would rely on the brand and trust the firm. "You'll see with enough time," he explained, "accounts will start opening."

Todd also said one other thing I would never forget: "We don't split atoms or land people on the moon here. There is a process, and like selling soap or any other product, if you are willing to put the time in and have the right, resilient personality, you will succeed."

He was right. I started opening accounts. It was an incredibly painful, yet positive experience. I was learning how to hunt and fish. After this experience I could be dropped anywhere in the world and I would be able to figure out a way to find and cultivate new clients. Sure, there were painful and unsettling moments. I couldn't bring myself to make certain calls, and sometimes I was filled with dread. It was classic sales with all of the uncertainty. When I finally broke through it, though, my self-assurance and self-confidence were immediately boosted.

Within a year, I had gone from unemployed to panicked to self-confident. It became clear that I was doing a good job and was carving a successful career for myself at Goldman. All professionals should vigilantly check in on their progress. Ask yourself about your current job: Is it opening up a future for you, where you can aspire to become a leader? Is there opportunity for growth and development? In today's environment just having a job makes most people quite grateful. The experience is secondary, the job is primary—any job. This isn't acceptable. Find one where you are thrown into the deep end of the pool. Once there, just hold your breath and laugh off the people who are trying to push your head underwater. If the firm you are at is any good, those types of people will eventually be weeded out.

■■■

By late 1995, I had over 300 clients and was generating $4.5 million in gross commissions. That was netting me—at the age of 31—over $1 million a year. Back then we were in a glorious bull market and I was a top producer. I had the opportunity to meet with Steve Ballmer, Maria and Bobby Shriver, Bill Anders the astronaut, and countless others. I was a Goldman Sachs PCS guy. "PCS" stood for Private Client Services because Securities Sales wasn't Goldman enough. Now it is known by most people as Private Wealth Management.

Despite all of my immaturity and restlessness I had no desire to leave Goldman Sachs for a competitor. There were countless stories of brokers selling their books to Lehman or to Donaldson, Lufkin & Jenrette (DLJ) or to First Boston for 125 to 150 percent of their gross—that's how Wall Street firms poach employees from each other. They give a broker like I was an up-front bonus equal to or more than several times an entire year's gross. The fine print reminds you that it is actually a loan that's only satisfied after you spend a certain number of years with the company. That always seemed short-sighted to me. I believed Goldman was the best and I didn't want to be seen as a person with a wandering eye.

Perhaps the best piece of career advice that I have learned over the years is to sit tight. Don't job-hop. Warren Buffett often counsels young professionals to have patience and perspective. After all, it takes many years (Buffett says 20) to build a reputation and many years to create a fabulous business. John Weinberg concurs, saying that a resume packed with job moves is a sign that someone couldn't dedicate themselves to a singular focus or they lacked the ability to ride through the ups and downs. Michael Dell has said during his speeches, "Don't day-trade your career." In other words, if you have a good thing going, stay at it and try to build upon it. Most of the people I know who are incredibly successful on Wall Street or in other professions have had the perseverance, patience, and controlled ambition to stay in one place.

But there are always exceptions in life, and in this case it's called the *passion* exception.

■■■

After seven years at Goldman, the paycheck, the status, the rubbing elbows with some of the wealthiest and smartest people in America wasn't enough. I know, it sounds strange, maybe even a little bit crazy, maybe even a bit hypocritical, but I had a passion to start my own business, and the timing and business partner seemed so right.

So, in 1996, I invoked the passion exception and I left Goldman. I'd had a burning desire since my first paper route to run my own business. Up until the moment I left, I was an entrepreneur in my own mind. Once in a while people would tell me I was crazy. "How could you leave such a good thing like the career that you are building at Goldman Sachs?" If I was after money and status then it probably was a bad career move, but I was after something more: I was trying to realize my dreams and attempting to fulfill some of my personal goals. My moral compass was changing its direction.

Before I graduated from law school, I made a list. Near the top: Create a business from scratch and run it successfully. That was the essence of the American Dream for me. Goldman? That was a wonderful place, they did almost everything right. The legendary Richard Menschel, who ran the Equities Division before he retired in 1987, said, "Anthony you will love us more after you leave us, especially after a few years have gone by." He was so right.

But for now, it was time to be true to myself. I had always wanted something that was my own.

How would I get it? The solution to my problem—at least this particular one—was in my past, back to Sol Gittleman's Yiddish literature course. Remember, Gittleman had helped me get into Tufts in exchange for taking his class and making him proud. Some of the basic wisdom of that single semester has become a lifelong guide for me.

Yiddish literature had fabulous lessons embedded in each of the stories. It was basically all about a commitment to family and culture, staying true to your roots, and keeping hope alive. Specifically, here are some of Gittleman's lessons from Yiddish literature:

- Be nice to your parents.
- Stick together.
- Work hard in school.
- Keep your religious faith and be true to your culture.
- Don't be too big for your britches.
- Fear authority, particularly the czarist police.
- Stand with your neighbor; share and bake bread.
- Cherish your family.
- Make a better life for your children.
- And children, make your parents proud.
- And for the modern era: Call your mother! She worries.

For me, those rules add up to one basic thing: Know thyself.

Having done some soul-searching, I knew then that I had a burning desire to run my own business. Even back at Harvard Law, my first-year paper detailed the best way to set up a sole proprietorship. Some of the people in my family have started and run their own businesses. My uncle had a motorcycle shop. One of my cousins has a deli and another has an auto glass shop. It was in my DNA.

Alex P. Keaton's wisdom notwithstanding, for me, money was no longer enough. I could have stayed at Goldman, hung around for the IPO (I never thought I had a chance to be partner at Goldman), and probably made enough money to retire. Even without making partner at Goldman, a professional career there was still a great path to financial wealth. Check personal ego, cash check. In this case, greed didn't overcome my unrelenting desire to own my own business. And who really wants to retire, anyway?

■■■

But there's another reason why I left. After all, a broker at Goldman is a bit of an entrepreneur and sole proprietor. Until, that is, the firm wants you to conform to something else. Now, I am all for the subordination of ego for the betterment of the firm. I played a lot of team sports as a kid and understood well that the whole was greater than the sum of its separate parts.

But remember, they had bounced me once, and there was no guarantee I wasn't going to get bounced again. One of my few tangible gifts is that I have a reasonable amount of self-awareness. Even at 32 I knew I didn't have the DNA for the place. There were people who enjoyed having me around, but there was always a lecture coming or some sort of eye roll.

But the real difficulty for me was the personality-ectomy that happened to Goldman guys. To be fair, a lot of people who work at Goldman Sachs don't need the personality transformation. In fact, many seem born for the job. For them, it was easy to be part of the team, I imagine, when you'd been playing on it since your blue-blazered prep school days. But I was clearly different than the people there.

The Scaramucci family affairs weren't at country clubs. They were at Sunday dinners. They were loud, raucous, fun, and loving. Nothing was buttoned up, including our shirts. To this day, when I enter a room, people know. There are hugs and loud greetings. It is me. It is my people. And it's nothing I wanted to lose. Realness, closeness, drama, hugging, laughing (hardest at yourself), eating, being loud, all of this stuff is so me. This didn't fit so well at Goldman. I am okay with it, but people should know that you can be all of those things and still be smart and professional. You can work hard and play hard. Brains come in all packages, even, in my case, as part of a guy who has taken disco dance lessons.

I enjoy authenticity, being myself, and getting some laughs when I'm in a room full of people. Don't believe me? Here's proof.

In early 2009, I gave a speech to a Jewish community group in Florida. The community's very real wounds from the Bernie Madoff scandal were still fresh. They had invested their money with one of their own and been betrayed. Family fortunes had been lost, futures blown apart, and some very worthwhile causes left penniless. That said, everyone needs a laugh. So I gave the crowd a bit of off-color financial advice: Always invest with an Italian. Italians like cash businesses. He'll only steal as much as he can fit in the trunk of his car in cash. If Madoff got $50 billion, the average Italian could probably only fit $2 million in the trunk of a black Lincoln. They'd be much better off.

C'mon now, it's a joke. The crowd loved it. It was like turning down a pressure gauge on their very real fears and anxieties. They relaxed and they were now open to hearing about my business. I felt their pain, made a wisecrack at my own expense, and got their attention. At Goldman, I couldn't have made that crack. I couldn't have been one of Oliver Stone's technical advisers or shot a small role in the movie *Wall Street: Money Never Sleeps*. No way could I have attended the Allen & Company media conference in Sun Valley, or the World Economic Forum in Davos.

But I'm getting ahead of myself. The bottom line is that after seven years with the company, I had done some soul-searching, recalled the distilled lesson from Sol's Yiddish class, and I realized I no longer wanted to be the total company man who concealed his spunk, censored his wisecracks, and succumbed to upper management's every wish and demand. I didn't want to morph my personality or polish away my rough edges. There isn't enough money to make me do that, and quite frankly, I couldn't have succeeded any other way.

We all aspire to things. I liked how I felt coming home to Long Island for school breaks and telling people I was at Tufts or Harvard. I liked going to parties and telling people I worked at Goldman (it used to make friends at Lehman grind their teeth; the Goldman guys used to call Lehman "the SchLehm"). But that's not who I was. You have to remember that those great places will become greater if your true gifts shine. They don't need another well-educated guy in khakis and a WASPy haircut marching in lockstep. Look at Goldman: Built by World War II vets, brought public by an unabashed Christian Scientist and environmentalist, and now run by a rough-and-tumble commodities trader from Brooklyn. And yet, in the ranks, guys look askance at the genuine.

Want to really succeed? Don't be like the people you think you want to be. Be yourself and the world will want to be with you.

■■■

Having said all that, I think that part of what has made Goldman great is the ability of its best people to form a collective consciousness. So my discussion here is in no way meant to be critical. The firm has thrived on its ability to create a one-firm, one-organization ethos. My early career greatly benefited from this as Goldman bankers were willing to cross-sell private banking products. This was something that most other firms found very difficult; they would rather not cross-sell and let someone else win the business. Silly. Goldman guys just got it. I will confess that when I started a firm I immediately started implementing many of the Goldman ideas as it relates to culture. So I hope it's clear that I loved the place even though I left it.

So, again, why did I leave? Why not fight it out and leave *my* mark on the venerable firm?

Simple: I knew what my meaning was in life. I wanted to be an entrepreneur and surround myself with people who dared to be themselves and not conform to a set culture. I wasn't as interested in dusting someone else's marble statue, no matter how lucrative. Carve my own rock, make $0 to $1 million. Dust someone else's rock, make $750,000 but don't fulfill my passion. (Note to readers: Those dollar figures are in 1989 dollars and pre–Wall Street ridiculous boom; now add zeroes.) It wasn't that I thought the grass was going to be greener; it was just that the manure that fed that grass was something I wanted to roll in. Gordon Gekko would be so appalled.

More generally, at some point you have to ask yourself who you are and, if you had no fear, what you would try to be. I am very proud that when I left Goldman, it wasn't to join a competitor. I left ultimately to try to become one of the people Goldman guys actually respect, the people around the globe whom they bow and cater to and generally live to serve: a client. No one has ever bowed to me though, and I like it like that.

■■■

I had wanted to be an entrepreneur for many years. There's a pride that goes into ownership, and the ability to attempt to control one's destiny, that was important to me.

There was also an element of owning something on your own that seemed, from a distance, special. Up close, I can say now, it's even more special. I often ask recruits: "Do you want to be a part of something where you can impact the culture or where the culture impacts you? Are you a capitalist or a capital-artist?"

Capital-artist. That's a great word. To be a capital-artist is to be a creator, a business builder.

Michael Dell, Bill Gates, Jeff Bezos, Pierre Omidyar. These are the Hall of Famers from my generation. If business is a blank canvas and your mind and environment are the brush, will you create something or leave it the same as it was before you arrived?

How people use computers all over the world changed permanently when Gates, then Dell, got into the business. And when Bezos left the comfy confines of hedge fund D. E. Shaw to start an online bookstore, others probably thought he was a little crazy or, in the best case, that he'd have an interesting couple of years and then come back to finance. We all know how that worked out. Amazon started with doors over sawhorses as desks and office furniture. Amazon now has a $50 billion-plus market cap. The book industry, the music business—heck, even the companies who sell appliances—will never be the same, all because one short, kind of nerdy bald guy decided he wanted to start an online bookstore. (I hope I am not being too critical of Jeff. Perhaps he looked nerdier than he is, the same way I started out guido.) These kinds of stories are powerful in the most real way I can imagine.

Quite frankly, I wanted a powerful story. I just wanted to leave *something* behind, great or otherwise. I wanted the journey.

In fact, I wanted it so badly that I was overconfident and at the same time wildly fearful. I'd gone from the safety of college campuses straight into the established arms of Goldman, where I didn't even have to sharpen a pencil.

Still, I left Goldman, with my new partner, Andrew K. Boszhardt Jr. on Friday, November 29, 1996. I took a pay cut from over a million dollars a year to a base pay of $240,000 (a lot of dough by any standard, especially in 1996, but nonetheless a significant difference with potential for failure). When I left, my direct boss, David Henle, said: "Well, now you are going to see how hard it is to manage people. You gave me a hard time, and now you will know the other side!" (Years later, during a lunch with David and in the midst of some staff turnover, I asked him to lift the curse.)

That weekend I was overwhelmed with angst and anxiety as a wave of what-ifs attacked. I had the stress flu. There is no vaccine for the stress flu, only experience. Fred Smith, the founder of FedEx, once said if he knew how hard it was going to be to be an entrepreneur he would probably have never tried it. Amen to that.

On December 2, 1996, Andy and I opened the doors of Oscar Capital, our first hedge fund. Oscar was derived from the first syllables of Boszhardt and Scaramucci. It was Boscar without the 'b.' There was no Uncle Oscar and no, we weren't related to the hot dog company or the Sesame Street grouch.

Andy was a brilliant maverick. He was a few years older than me and was a classic iconoclast. I looked up to him and admired his classic

Midwestern common sense, but also his aggression. He proved to be a great partner and teacher. He was empowering, generous, and charitable, and helped me deal with whatever fears and insecurities I had at the time. Above all, he was all about succeeding and sharing, a belief that I have taken from him.

The first few days of Oscar Capital started with Alan Greenspan's December 1996 "Irrational Exuberance" speech. The market took a dive, and I remember being on the phone with one of my Goldman colleagues who was still safely ensconced in the firm and thinking about how scared I was.

Robert K. Steel, a famous Goldman Sachs partner who ultimately became Under Secretary for Domestic Finance at the U.S. Department of the Treasury and the last CEO of Wachovia, said to my partner and me: "You left Goldman to become two guys and a dog." He was dead wrong—we didn't have a dog. Essentially, we were starting a *de novo* business in the classic sense. We sat in a small room with a few computers and we began mailing out documents. There were so many things to do that had been done for us while we were at Goldman and now we had to do them ourselves. We also had no clients. So we called upon old Goldman clients and potential new ones to invest in our hedge fund or into our separately managed account business.

We also didn't know about some of the administrative parts of the business. Some things I didn't know when we started to put together Oscar Capital:

- The cost of tech support.
- The cost of rubber bands.
- The cost of the Pitney Bowes machine—whatever that was.
- The cost of color copier cartridges.

Notice the common word, *cost*.

Then there was the paperwork. Trying to determine health care insurance for employees was among the hardest work I'd ever done. Now, don't get me wrong. I did have a leg up. Doors had opened to me because I was a Goldman guy, pure and simple. Now I had to tell people I met that I was part of Oscar Capital—what was that?

By January 1997, the money started coming in and we were in the process of creating a business. I can remember leaving the office at the end of January and thinking that it might all just work out. We were performing well. We had clients and we were doing a good job on the operational side of the business, something that we really didn't know much about several short weeks ago.

But this venture could have had a much different beginning that could have actually made it its ending. What if the market had crashed while we were trying to get our business off the ground? Imagine if our start date was September 10, 2001, or September 14, 2008? A financial crisis or tragic global event is frankly nothing that you can truly plan for, and there's only so much that you can control. Essentially, there is luck in the process, and thankfully we were lucky. The world was to stay irrational and exuberant.

I can remember when curious Goldman private bankers would come up to our office and attempt to live vicariously through us. When I would give them a tour of our small office, I would say, "Guys do you want to take a look at my summer home?" Then I would take them down the hall, open the closet door, and show them the server farm that was supporting our computers and market data. "There it is, my summer home—or at least, the money I would have put towards it. If you want your summer home to be in a nondescript closet in a nondescript office then you, too, should leave Goldman." We didn't get many takers.

■■■

Starting a business like I did led to instant maturity, self-reliance, and the development of adaptive critical thinking. All of the things I always wanted. It's great for some people who want to be in a big organization to work at a place like Goldman, but I always wanted to see if I could hunt and fish on my own with a small pack of zealots. It seemed a simple equation to me: Control your own destiny or someone else will. Most men live lives of quiet desperation. If I was going to be desperate it was going to be loud. At times it hasn't been easy, but it has been a very passionate, wonderful career.

One of the best days was on December 31, 1997. We were about to close our first full year in business and our fund was up an astounding 81 percent. It had been a magical first year in which everything went our way. When it turned it was abrupt, sobering, and painful, but on that day it was entrepreneurial bliss. Since then my career has taken me all over the world and it has allowed me to meet friends and establish business contacts on most of the major continents (still working on Africa and Antarctica).

So why was I successful? What makes someone able to succeed at something that's important to them? In my mind, it all boils down to confidence and perception—and a little bit of luck. Don't allow yourself to be shackled to your own self-consciousness or inhibitions. In fact, bizarrely, it is those of us who are willing to go out on a limb and project a confident, open, and in my case, even somewhat goofy personality to magnetize others. It is very tough for people, especially young people, to understand this, and some people never get there, but the propulsion of your personality will improve your happiness and your success. So let it hang out. Dare to be different.

Why be like others? Conformity and comfort go hand in hand. Lack of conformity creates self-consciousness and fear that you will be ostracized socially. I never belonged to a fraternity in college and I have never been overly tempted by peer pressure. Have the courage to be yourself; don't follow the crowd. Think about the people who you read about in history or those on the Forbes 400. I am often confused when I look at some of the CEOs who are interviewed on CNBC today. They all look the same and talk the same. Founders don't. They all look a little nuts. Steve Jobs, nuts. Bill Gates, nuts. Sergey and Larry, two nuts. Jeff Immelt, not so much.

Most of the CEOs I just named are gifted individualists who took a varied but independent path to their success. Even Michael Dell—for all of his quietness and soberness, underneath it all you can see his intense, seething passion. I remember the first time I met him. I was 28 at the time and he was 27. I did everything right and he did everything wrong. I listened to my parents. I finished college and law school, and like every other neurotic Alex P. Keaton-wannabe who wanted to be rich, I headed to Wall Street. In many ways, my decision to go to law school and eventually Goldman was very conforming and indicative of my goal to make money. Not Michael—he dropped out of college and never fulfilled his parents' dream of following his brother to med school. In 1992, my net worth was *minus* $100,000; I think Michael's at the time was $430 million. He did everything wrong except the right thing. He rightfully followed his dream and his passionate idea that he could compete against IBM. Talk about audacity, yet Michael was an accomplice in knocking IBM out of the personal computer business.

Listen to others for advice, but ultimately follow only yourself. There is a compass inside you, anchoring you to your future. Stay true to it.

■■■

Andrew and I sold Oscar Capital to money management giant Neuberger Berman in 2001. I was glad to be part of a quality operation and still able to maintain control over the business. Then Lehman Brothers bought Neuberger in 2003 and things changed. Lehman, as I described earlier, was a place run by a small cohort that was loyal to a fault, dead-set in their beliefs about what made the company tick, and reluctant to let others in the circle. It worked for them for quite a long time as Lehman thrived as a perennial underdog. It felt strong and confident in 2003, but when I saw the Lehman management style in action, I began thinking about my next entrepreneurial venture.

If you don't change for yourself, the world does it for you. I wasn't afraid of change, for sure, and Wall Street was certainly changing.

Maybe Lehman should have been less afraid of change, less afraid to sell when times were good, less afraid to refuse to follow Wall Street into a game of Russian roulette with leverage and hyperactive trading.

I don't know. But I knew what I wanted, and that was to start another enterprise. It was time for another mission. I was armed with a lot more experience and a more direct line to helping other people redirect their moral compass. Still, going out on my own again was scary. Building something from nothing is always a risk—even riskier than sticking around Lehman, believe it or not—but for me, it was riskier not to try again.

This time, I wanted my business to help people do what I love to do: start businesses and help them grow. In 2005, after months of studying new business ideas, I decided on building a money management firm that was dedicated to backing emerging managers and giving clients a piece of ownership in those sorts of businesses. SkyBridge is now a recognized name in the hedge fund incubation business.

For me, taking an idea from nothing to something is the crux of it. After all, I am a *capital-artist*. My canvas just happens to be Wall Street and my brushes are the money managers for whom SkyBridge raises capital.

I had no idea whether SkyBridge was going to succeed, but at the age of 41 I knew that I had enough experience and energy to do my very best to make it happen.

At SkyBridge, I try to pass along the values that I learned from Sol Gittleman's Yiddish literature class to the managers we choose to fund. We support each other and stick together; we work hard and push to make ourselves better; we know not to confuse brains with a bull market so few of us get too confident; and I try to use my life experiences to create a better business. Essentially, we treat the members of the SkyBridge team like a family—we worry about them, how they are performing, what they need to perform better, and how they treat their clients. And one thing's for sure: We are mentoring and training many people on Wall Street as they grow their hedge funds. No Gekkos allowed.

So, unlike my friend Alex P. Keaton, I have found my moral compass. (Who knows, maybe Alex grew up and found his moral compass; or maybe he grew up to be like Gordon Gekko.) I realized that I need people. I need to spend my days helping people make their dreams real, not cobbling together deals for a faceless corporation and carrying the flag for a firm that makes money merely for the sake of making money. I need to be true to myself, not just take a job because of the paycheck that accompanies it. Gordon Gekko would laugh and probably throw me out of his limo. Isn't that the best place to be?

Chapter 4

Capital

Real Wealth

Anthony, leave money on the table for your partners. Not only will you be very rich, but you will be very happy.

—*Li Ka-shing*

I was half-asleep in a Hong Kong hotel room on Sunday morning in 1998 when the telephone rang. A colleague, Moses Tsang, was on the line. "Wake up and get a suit on," he said. "I am going to take you to see the old man."

The "old man" was Li Ka-shing, the great property tycoon known across Asia and the world for his investment savvy, entrepreneurship, and leadership skills. In Hong Kong, the people call him "Superman" because he is among the most connected people in Asia and has given the public the perception that he has the Midas touch. He has great influence throughout China and in the global markets, and has a vast network of people on whom he relies. A long-term, patient investor, he is often referred to as the Warren Buffett of the East. Or maybe he's so good that Buffett is the Li Ka-shing of the West.

Oscar Capital was two years old and Moses Tsang, who once ran a large slice of Goldman's Asian business, was helping us make it bigger. He had retired from Goldman in 1994. In April 1998, I took a two-week trip to Hong Kong to meet people and build our business. Moses had a great relationship with Mr. Li and he was very happy to extend that relationship to my new firm. I was ecstatic.

When we arrived at Li's offices, we were greeted in the lobby, first by warm hostesses, who were diminutive and gracious, and then by large muscular bodyguards who were cold and observant. In 1996, one of Mr. Li's children was kidnapped by notorious gangster "Big Spender" Cheung Chi Keung, and released after a reported ransom of HK$1 billion was paid. With this event taking place just a few years ago, these muscle-men were hired to be vigilant and protective. Since they knew Moses, they relaxed once we entered the building. We were then whisked up to the top floor of the fairly nondescript building, which conveyed the modesty that Li, Asia's richest man, revered. We were taken into a private conference room and served hot tea while we waited.

Shortly thereafter "KS," as his friends call him, walked in. Having played a round of golf on the mainland earlier in the morning, he was showered and fresh.

We exchanged pleasantries. "So, tell me Anthony," he began. "What do you think of the U.S. market?" He asked this question in a way that made it clear he wanted to glean the information. He was soft-spoken, kind, and courtly. It was hard not to be impressed by his demeanor.

Oy. Here I was with one of the most influential people in the world and he was asking me to render an opinion on the market. I was eager to impress him with my knowledge and erudition, but I fought down my youthful enthusiasm because I knew that if I did the majority of the talking, this meeting would end with little impact. And really, what could I possibly tell one of the richest people in the history of the planet about the stock market?

I worked up my nerve and responded honestly: "Mr. Li, forgive me, but markets rise and markets fall. My opinion will be mere speculation.

If it isn't too much of an imposition, I would like to ask you a question. I'm turning 35 this year and you are about to turn 70. What can you tell me about *your* life that I can take with me for the rest of *my* life?"

He paused and then proceeded to tell us a short version of his life story. Central to it was that he is a contrarian by nature. When others were fearful, he was courageous. We learn so often that one of the essential keys to dramatic success is the ability to see things before others do. Li is such a visionary.

In 1967, there were riots and protests on the Hong Kong island. People feared Mao Tse-tung was going to take over Hong Kong and ignore the British-based laws related to property rights—much like Castro would do in Cuba and Lenin did in Russia five decades earlier.

Land values plummeted. Li aggressively acquired real estate at distressed prices, correctly assessing that Mao needed a free-market trading port to continue the commercial flow of goods. Mao, he assessed, was just too smart to make that mistake.

Li made a killing. He grew up on the mainland, moved to the rock known as Hong Kong (which means "fragrant harbor"—something years ago in the water, perhaps algae, gave the area a flowery smell), and then built a plastic flower company. He became an exporter. He quickly and intuitively realized that the panicked selling would abate. When the panic ended he was slowly becoming one of the largest landholders in Hong Kong. He was able to take profits from his buildings and develop telecommunications, energy, and eventually Internet ventures. He was a deal maker and capable of making decisions that others wouldn't have the guts to take on.

While he was explaining some of his deals and his thought process, the true pearl of his wisdom emerged:

Anthony, leave money on the table for your partners. Not only will you be very rich, you will be very happy. If you allow your partners to benefit from the deal, they always come back and want to do business with you. There will never be a shortage of opportunity.

It is the man who goes to the table to ask and squeeze for the last nickel who is never happy. Do you know why? It is because that person leaves the table, typically getting the nickel, but then hates himself for not asking for two nickels. As a result, he is never happy.

These words rang like a bell in my head. How many people do you know who are so rich, yet so miserable? When I thought about it, there seemed to be an entire social class on Wall Street that fit this description—and they were always striving, reaching, and pushing for more and more even though they never seemed to feel any more content.

Part of Li's formula was to not be the terribly ruthless, venomous Gordon Gekko of the 1980s who thought every deal was a zero-sum game. Do you remember that scene from the original *Wall Street* film? In wondering how much is enough, the greedy Gekko told his young protégé, Bud, "It's not a question of enough, pal. It's a zero-sum game—somebody wins, somebody loses. Money itself isn't lost or made, it's simply transferred from one perception to another."

In this scene, Gekko is shown as a greedy mogul who always thinks he is negotiating with an opponent and needs to play hardball so that he alone comes out on top. People like him are always struggling to squeeze the last dollar out of a deal or to exact terms from the other side that leaves them hurting. "Let me see how badly I can take advantage of the person across the table. I am macho and I need to prove my superiority over the person—let me squeeze and chisel."

These Gekko-like rogues run rampant on Wall Street. In fact, to some people, if you are not like this, it's a sign of weakness—like you are a goody two-shoes or a wimp who doesn't belong in the game. They justify their behavior by saying business is business and personal is personal. They separate the two in their minds in order to rationalize their behavior. And they share a common characteristic: They are universally restless and unfulfilled. Was it because their mothers didn't love them enough? Someone take their milk money in third grade? Who knows? But there is something deeply rooted in their resentment of humanity, and it's a revenge sort of thing: "I was hurt once—now I am going to take it out on you and the rest of the world."

They have respect only for other life losers like themselves. Yes, you can be become very rich and be a life loser. These short-term winners will typically get rich, but in the long run they are losers, tossing away their souls and reputations. When they fall, people step away from them (more on them a bit later).

The meeting with Mr. Li was one of the better meetings of my career. We got a mandate from a great man and his institution to manage some money, but the learning experience had a far greater value. He was gracious with his time and sincere, while I absorbed his words like a sponge. The smartest among us practice listening. Hard to learn when your lips are flapping—so learn when to keep your mouth shut! We all have the impulse to prove our knowledge, but it is always better to listen and learn, especially when we are in the presence of greatness.

But, more important, he gave me a tremendous lesson about wealth and its relation to happiness at exactly the right time in my life.

■■■

Do you think that leaving money on the table for a business partner— walking away with less than you could have—is a strange practice for a business icon? Watched enough *Apprentice* to think it may even be a crazy idea for a man who has made billions in a region where rules are hard to come by—and people who follow them, even harder?

Yet Gordon Gekko's *Wall Street* mantra of "Greed is good" couldn't be further from the truth, especially for those as vastly wealthy as Li. For him, his journey and his life experience have been about creating other intrinsic forms of capital.

Capital is not only cash, stocks, and real estate. Capital is any asset that you can store and rely upon, and it comes in many forms. There is capital in economic terms, which consists of investment assets, cash, and things like equipment on a company's balance sheet. There is also human capital, which is made up of those who work with you. When you establish healthy win-win relationships with people, your capital account grows and can earn you a lot of dough. But accumulating enough of any of those can only happen if you trust that your actions are worthwhile no matter what the return.

In Li's case, his capital consisted of a set of values and his ability to value relationships. His philosophy may not always work over the short term, but look at the full canvas of his life and you can see he has painted a masterpiece. He is a capital-artist who employs the principles of kindness and fairness—betting that they will always win out over thuggish hardball.

It is too idealistic to suggest that one should never assert toughness, but to do so for the mere sake of doing it is harmful to long-term relationships. I am confident that Li has had his share of tough negotiations and I am not here to glorify him. He has earned, however, a reputation of being someone that many people want to do business with. Some will never, ever get this. In fact, they'll laugh at the namby-pamby rhetoric. They'll attribute it to naiveté, a false understanding of human nature and hope. They'll also do their best to take advantage of those who actually believe in leaving money on the table. They'll say, "Generosity and the attempt to build long-term relationships are silly." They believe life and work are a zero-sum game and they need to get everything they can out of a deal.

I would love to be able to tell you to stop doing business with these sorts of people at all costs. In an ideal world this would be the best advice, but I am too practical to suggest something like that. People of this ilk are unavoidable and lurk around the corridors of most businesses. Just be on guard, call it out when you can, and be ready to take advantage of their greed.

■■■

Li has certain wisdom and understands there are two types of bank accounts—one is filled with karma. It is natural for most people secure enough with themselves to be generating this type of karma. Now, I'm just a Catholic kid from Long Island, so I may not have a deep Eastern philosophical understanding of the term. Here, however, is my home-spun take: Karma is the spirit of good feeling that is created by your actions and deeds, the circulatory system for goodwill. I am not sure why, but most of us are wired to give. The pleasure we receive from the process of helping others is among the deepest we know, and it will also do amazing things for your life and career.

Be it a small gesture or a large one, everything counts toward the karmic bank deposits. Dickens identified this in his timeless classic *A Christmas Carol*. Scrooge's years of misery and greed were erased with the joy of helping the crippled boy, Tiny Tim. His story was a plea for those with plenty not to turn their backs on the lower classes and the disadvantaged. Generosity engages the human spirit. It has an almost therapeutic effect. Scrooge at least got it and found his soul in the end.

In my career I have met plenty of Jacob Marleys, the devilish part-ner of Scrooge—callous and soulless without a remote possibility of redemption. They are smug in their conviction that they are doing the right thing. They think it is all about Darwinian survival, pit-ting themselves against others. The Marleys dodge charitable giving and leaving money on the table unless it selfishly provides them with something.

In my career I have also met plenty of anti-Marleys. A friend of mine, Chris Quackenbush, was so taken with this story that he started the Jacob Marley Foundation. He dedicated himself to anonymous and open giving. He taught children to read, brought them to Mets games, helped to build homeless shelters, supported health care and projects, and all sorts of other good stuff. He died in the South Tower of the World Trade Center on September 11, 2001. Yet his good works live forever in all of the people whom he has positively touched.

Larger than life and with such a winning personality, you just sort of knew that when it was time for him to leave the planet he would go in a big way. And he did. He is missed and stilled loved.

When the Marleys I know on Wall Street die, no one will miss them, let alone memorialize them.

My prescription for finding your fortune while not losing your soul: Give time and money to causes you believe in, and teach others who can benefit from your wisdom and experience. Generosity is a healing agent for all of humanity, and an equalizer that helps to make society fairer. We don't have to be mega-rich to be generous. Although those who are grab the headlines, it is the common, everyday generosity that sustains the world.

That runs a bit counter to how most people think of the wealthy, especially those who are wealthy themselves. F. Scott Fitzgerald wrote that the rich are different from you and me. While there might be some truth in that, take it from a person who deals with them every day: They aren't *that* different. Some are gracious and kind; some are spoiled and entitled. If you happen to feel entitled then it is quite likely that you can't feel gratitude. If you can't feel gratitude then you will never fully appreciate what you have.

Wealth, I have observed, is a personality-force multiplier. If you are a good guy to begin with, you will become a better guy. If you are a bad guy when you start out, you're not going to get any nicer. There are some very generous people in the world who are quite poor. We very rarely hear of those. There are some very generous people who are mega-rich, and their names (like Buffett, Gates, and Bloomberg) are everywhere. These good people who happen to be super rich can make exponential differences with their wealth. But there are also people who are quite bad, and the richer they get, the more their venality gets exposed. Make sure that, rich or poor, you have the right habits, ones that you can be proud of.

Recognize as quickly as you can that wherever you are in life and no matter how disappointed you may be by some of the vagaries that you have experienced, it is a joy to be alive. Be grateful and express it. Be generous and forward thinking.

This advice also translates into the workplace. The best bosses want their employees and colleagues to do well. How often do we experience the boss or the leader who cares only about his own career? Don't be that guy. Want to attract the best and the brightest people to your endeavor? Let it be known that you will promote their careers.

One of my mentors at Goldman Sachs promoted several very young people into the partnership class ahead of their time. His name was John McNulty. He was trying to send a message to people inside the firm: "If you work for me I am going to promote you and your career. I am going to help you reach your goals." I was always impressed with this and looked up to John. He was brilliant and he had great emotional intelligence. Unfortunately, we lost him to a heart attack at the age of 53 in 2005; he was a great role model. Earning that reputation is the surest magnet for talent.

■ ■ ■

Just as there is an ethical way to attract and grow capital, there is also a morally corrupt way. And I am sure that there are some Mr. Gekkos reading this book right now. If you are that nasty, selfish person trying to squeeze the last nickel from things and get a little bit lucky, you will likely get rich. Life is unfair and, like it or not, bad guys too often win. The financial world has a tendency to reward and reinforce sociopathic and destructive behavior.

The internal sales job inside the sociopath's head goes something like this: "Society is rewarding my abhorrent tendencies through my wealth; therefore, I will continue on course." This is the worst part of success, and this is how people turn into miserable millionaires. Think about it: If you have to be an avaricious ass to make your money, okay, now you are king of the mountain—but let me ask you, who are you going to share your success with? Sycophants and suck-ups?

Sure, you will always find someone to be with; there are a lot of people out there who are fixated on money or luxury. The term *gold digger* is no joke. Be a jerk, get rich, hang out with jerks, be miserable, never really know why you're miserable when you have everything on your want list, and die empty. That would be such a waste of life and talent. And like it or not, riches can go away and status can disappear in an instant. Think about the evildoers who fall: Their false friends always evacuate. Be the type of person who will make true friends, supportive in thick and thin.

If you make it big, were born into it, or are currently big, ask yourself a really tough question: Stripped of my wealth tomorrow, who will still be with me? And while you're asking yourself things, check in on how you treat people and whether you make them feel comfortable around you.

All human life deserves dignity and respect. Where we stand in life is often a by-product of luck. Sure, some of it is hard work, but did you pick your eye color, your skin color, your parents, or the location of your birth? What about your brain chemistry? If you didn't, then accept that a lot of things that happen are beyond your control. The same is true for the people in your life. We are all starting from different places and perspectives and we know intuitively that life is unfair. Yet if you are reading this book, chances are that life has been more than fair to you. Why do I say that? You likely live in an industrialized country and someone taught you to read; that is better than most who inhabit our world. So be your best, give, and share.

■ ■ ■

The concept of giving means many things, and little of it is linear. Think of it as taking a piece of the fire from your soul and using it to light the world. You have to give in such a way that you are not expecting anything in return except the satisfaction of having given and knowing that the gods (whichever ones you worship) are smiling down on you. And if you're an atheist, you intuitively know that you are wired to feel good when helping others—call it the Darwinian gene of needing each other for our own survival. No matter what you think about or believe in, giving will help you find a happier and more fulfilling life. It is inherently purposeful.

But I am not saying you should give to get things back. I am saying you should give because it's good for the soul and because it illustrates one of the most important qualities: Giving breeds trust and goodwill.

The word *trust* itself is one of the most powerful in our language (but not *the* most powerful—the most powerful word in the English language and a few other languages is *no*, but that's for another book). When I think of trust I think of the word *vulnerability*. If we can expose our vulnerabilities to another person, then right there is a pathway to trust. Giving without expectation—such as leaving money on the table for a partner—makes us all vulnerable. Will our partners try to take advantage of our goodwill? Will we be played the fool by a street beggar who will use the spare change we give him to get drunk instead of buying food? Will the woman we are dating think the flowers we send are a sign of being too smitten? Or will she just like them?

Vulnerability often is a sign of wisdom. It allows you to connect. Open up. Okay, my friends, here are some of my weaknesses:

- I fear heights (yet I don't fear flying—go figure).
- As for my appearance, I always wanted to be taller and thinner.
- New trouble comes up every day that I have to deal with.
- I avoid conflict, which has cost me money as I have been out-negotiated on some deals.
- I am a crowd-pleaser.

And no one is exempt. Here are a few vulnerabilities from successful friends of mine:

- My one eye turns in.
- My relationship with my parents isn't where it should be.

- I am recovering from drug or alcohol addiction.
- My dad abused me.

The point is, you know your vulnerabilities, and I know mine. Share them with someone you trust. Then you can move on from quiet self-consciousness to a life where giving is simply a part of it. No obligation; just the daily recognition that we are tethered to each other on this planet.

Throughout my life and career I have looked up to the people who can do this. Only later in life did I see one of the best examples of a person who is open and shares all her vulnerabilities: Oprah

What make Oprah so special? Well, she may have risen to fame as a talk show host but she bleeds. She is real. She is open, has empathy, and combines charity with her work. Oprah . . . people trust Oprah.

Wall Streeters should watch Oprah. When Oprah looks at a guest on her show, her demeanor gives off not a shred of judgment. There is no arrogance in her message. The message feels like: "I actually understand you and I understand pain. I am a real person and I want to share my life with you and help you to realize we are all in this together. I feel your pain."

She seems to recognize that we are all the same, that we've just had different circumstances bestowed on us. It's genuine, sincere, and not calculated or transparent. She loves life, had a bad childhood, and has had her weight plastered on the cover of every celebrity magazine on the rack. Her bottom line: Love life. Embrace it. She is powerful, for sure, but she is vulnerable, honest, and real, and a lot of her power starts there because it establishes a bond.

Now, I'm not suggesting that you should act like the typical guest on the Oprah or Dr. Phil show, having a daily cathartic moment with everyone you meet. You will know when the time is right to share a part of yourself. I am saying that healthy, open dialogue with people makes you *real* or *regular*. It also shows people that you are at ease with yourself and feel comfortable with your life story, or at least are somewhat at peace with it. It may take a while, and with certain people it may never happen. Yet the process of sharing vulnerability will open you to others and give them, too, an opportunity to open up.

I sometimes laugh out loud when I am having a conversation with someone who is trying to convince me that his life was written by a 1950s TV family sitcom screenwriter. All is perfect, no *dys* in front of the word *function*. Really? And I mean *really* in the way they say it on *Saturday Night Live*'s "Weekend Update." I mean really, your life is perfect? If you believe so, stay away from a lie detector test. However, if it's not perfect, always start from the side of gratitude, never bitterness.

■■■

It's interesting. Giving, confidence, and building trust all feed off each other. You want to know what makes it easier for me to give back? I've made my fortune and have the confidence that having created it once, if it all goes away, I can re-create it. I hope that doesn't come off as arrogant (even though I think it might). I really think that if you are being true to yourself in business the money will find you. The fact that I made it not as a swashbuckling investment banker or cold-blooded trader but, in the parlance of old Wall Street, as a customer's man, is indicative of my personality.

I see wealth developing like a meal at a better restaurant.

On the menu, there are appetizers: a new car, your first house. Then the main course: a McMansion and a ski house or beach getaway. Then there's dessert: an Amex Black Card and a private jet.

Okay, admittedly, I am eating off of this menu. I have a Porsche. I belong to a club that has a swimming pool that's heated at a temperature high enough to cook 100 pounds of linguini (Al Gore has one, too, and carbon offsets are a little offsetting!), and sometimes I use a share of a private jet. But there are times that I fly JetBlue for $400 because it's just not that important to me to parachute into a city on a private jet. I fill the car with super, but I also walk around my home and office shutting off lights that aren't being used. If I get a 15 percent off coupon I am going to use it. I am not going to do something extravagant just to prove that I can afford it, but I will do things that are if they provide me or someone I love with a great life experience. Yes, I have been on the VIP tour at Disney!

I've decided where to draw the lines in my life, especially in regard to wealth. For instance, I will not buy art. First off, I don't know much about it so it would be wasted on me. Second, and more important, it just feels like a wealth totem. Some people in my industry are accumulating art because they are lifelong collectors. These people are quite rare. Other people on Wall Street are buying art to prove to people that they have taste or money to burn.

Why art? There are a lot of psychological reasons and some of them probably make sense. I am sure there are sociologists who can come up with fancy answers and justifications, but I think the main reason why people acquire it if they are on Wall Street is so they can have something exclusive that none of their other rich friends can have. A typical rich person can bulk up on Mercedes, Rolex, Dom Perignon, and other sorts of luxury brands. The others are bummed out, though, because these items have effectively become a rich person's commodity and so they no longer feel unique or special. Yet with art, if it's an original, one-of-a-kind piece, that will be worth a lot to someone who wants things that others covet but can't have. It sort of goes like this: "You are worth a billion dollars and so am I, but I am the only one in the world who owns this particular Picasso. Eat your heart out and die." The rich love driving each other crazy with this sort of thing.

This reminds me of the scene in the first *Wall Street* movie when the seductive Darianne shows the naïve Bud Fox Gordon Gekko's exquisite art collection, which is full of rather unattractive paintings and sculptures that are priced high enough to "buy a penthouse on Park Avenue." I don't know about you, but I'd take the apartment or maybe do something more meaningful with my money.

Now, I am not denigrating those who collect, and I am probably a cretin for not understanding the whole thing. But it's just one more example of the height of Wall Street arrogance. In my opinion, there are very few things in life more vile than bearing witness to a smug, self-assured, though slightly insecure, arrogant fool who always wants to tell you about his Hinckley yacht or his Picasso. Instead, I choose to surround myself with people who, like me, choose to mentor young people, raise money to fight cancer, and, through their profession, develop intellectual capital. These things sometimes aren't super glamorous and haven't improved my social status, but I am actually doing something. Doing something worthwhile is the only way to be a role model, to inculcate your children (or anyone's children) with a passion to work, to serve, and to give back.

■■■

I always like it when my name comes up, when people talk about me. Those who tease tell me, "You don't care what they say, good or bad, as long as they are talking about you." Okay, so I am a bit of a diva. Yet the truth is I want the reaction from most people to be that I am generous, grounded, real, warm-hearted, and encouraging.

Having said all of that, it's not bad to have some enemies. In fact, your enemies—or even your *frienemies*—define you. I take great pride in the fact that I am not on the right side of everyone. More often than not, the reason someone doesn't like me is because of our diverging values, principles, or personalities. They may also be put off by my bluntness and tendency toward pomposity. I wear those adversaries like a badge of honor. The trick in dealing with these frienemies is not to stoop to their level. Trust me—as humans, that is no easy task.

I worked with a high-ranking executive at Lehman Brothers whose shortcomings could be used in an elite business school case study on why that firm really failed. He was one of the most difficult and insecure people I had come across in my career. He was always talking about his toys, yachts, cars, and house in the Hamptons. It was important that everyone who worked underneath him knew that he had dough and that if life was being judged by who has the most toys, he was winning. He was insecure about his education, uptight about his technical understanding of financial products, and would never stay in one area long enough to earn people's respect. He switched jobs in the firm every three years. Just as people were figuring out he was incompetent, he was moving to kiss butt in another area. He was the guy who returned the calls of his bosses but of few others.

I love SAT words, such as *obsequious*, *sycophantic*, and *toadying*. They are some of my favorites because they can be applied all over Wall Street. I actually tip my cap to those people who are good at it because it has made them millions of dollars. This particular guy probably never got a degree from college. No BA or BS, although he no doubt had a doctorate in a different sort of BS as well as in AK (if you can't figure out what AK is please go to our web site—this is a family book!). Guys who have PhDs in BS or AK love it when their subordinates suck up. Pass the barf bag.

I can't stand when people don't give it to me straight. None of us is perfect, and if I am doing something wrong, I want to hear about it so I can correct it. Not this guy, though. You couldn't tell him anything.

One day this quintessential yes-man brought me into his office and asked me why I thought he and I weren't getting along. I knew he was sensitive about his weight. He constantly talked about it and thought his life would be perfect if he could just lose 50 pounds. I still laugh at that. Nobody's life is perfect.

In any case, after he asked me why we weren't getting along, I said something that I still regret to this day: "Well, for starters, you like people to fawn over you and tell you things about yourself that aren't true."

"Like what?"

"Like, your triple chin looks like a double chin. That's something that I am never going to say to you."

In an instant, I stooped to this guy's level.

Okay, it felt good to say, but it was a dumb, horrible, mean, insensitive thing to do. It didn't help the situation. It probably put me closer to the door and to starting SkyBridge, but it was immature and uncalled for. Sure, he only cared about himself, his own personal vanity, and his status. Sure, he was a phony, but I stooped to his level and for that I feel bad.

There is an Italian expression that translates into, "Class is unlike water, you can't find it everywhere." Stay classy. I do not say that out of a sense of superiority but out of a sense of principle—one I sometimes need to remind myself of. You have to have a sense of what's important and do what you know is right.

One of my great mentors, Sol Gittleman, gave us a reading assignment that I still reflect upon often, even more than 25 years after I first read it. It was called the *Lottery Ticket*; it was written by Sholom Aleichem and was a beautiful and painful story. There was a proud father who was living in eastern Russia in a Jewish *shtetl*. Every day he would gather with his friends and they would share stories of their children. Eventually, these stories turned into *kvelling* episodes—that's Yiddish for bragging. And so they would sit there in the square and talk about their children—their daughters were pillars of rectitude and innocence, and each of their sons were the first coming of the Messiah. One father was particularly proud: His son's grades were so high that he was going to go to medical school. He was going to grow up to become a doctor. Ah yes, my son the doctor—that was the pinnacle of *nakhes* (honor) in the community.

But there's a twist: There was a quota for the Jewish students and only a few could get in. The son was rejected. He got the wrong lottery ticket. Thinking he would shine in his parents' eyes, he switched religions and became a Christian to get accepted. This, of course, was devastating to the father and the family since he abandoned his culture and religion in exchange for an earthly reward. Instead of honor there was shame. It was tough. There was no happy ending.

This parable taught me a valuable lesson that I pass on to you. Capital comes in many forms. It isn't just money. There are other things to bank and to transfer to others.

Accomplishments don't mean much if you leave big pieces of your soul behind. Stay true and always leave money on the table for your partners.

Chapter 5

Knowledge
Lessons from Unlikely Places

There is no better education than the one you got at Ghost.
                                                                          —Uncle Sal

There are many different ways to gain knowledge. Some of the most common are received from a formal education, reading, experience, and training. For me, I think that the way you grow up strongly alters the prism through which you look at life. Sometimes it helps that I can look at life through the lens of someone educated at Tufts and Harvard Law. Sometimes it helps even more, though, when I look at life as someone who spent his formative years in a motorcycle shop.

After my father's army enlistment was up, he and my mom went back to Port Washington, the town that my mother grew up in. My family had a small white house on the corner of Webster Avenue and Madison Street; it had three tidy bedrooms and three bathrooms. I shared a room with my older brother and all of us shared the upstairs bathroom. The best part of the house was its location next to the town's elementary school. Growing up near the Main Street School was terrific;

it was a short walk to school and had a gigantic playground with a large athletic field next to it. This was ideal for early morning football games.

Near the school and, on the southwest corner of Main Street—at number 194, to be exact—was Ghost Motorcycles, where I received some of the most integral lessons of my life. Yes, I've worked at Goldman, I went to Tufts and Harvard, but from the age of 13 to 19, I worked at Ghost and earned an SE—a degree in Street Education.

Every Saturday, the Ghost Motorcycle shop shattered the quiet suburban morning with the growling tumult of Hell's Angels, rich hobbyists, and any other type of biker you could imagine converging on the place. It always drew entertaining and interesting people, as motorcycles attract some of the widest spectrum and bandwidth of human beings.

It was a cultural icon for the area. In the 1960s it was an incredibly popular destination. In the 1970s it had a resurgence when the price of gas led to the rise of the miserly moped. Yet the town desperately tried to close it down. The locals hated the noise and everyone hated the element that was drawn to the shop. The town's politicians were always trying to find a new rule or ordinance that would force the shop to move out of the town. It was an eyesore and a place that had a very bad perception; many of my friends' parents could be overheard saying, "Stay away from Ghost." Everyone had a bad opinion of the place except for my family—probably because it was owned by my Uncle Sal.

My Uncle Sal earned the nickname "the Ghost" because that's how the local cops would refer to him on their radio as he flew past them on his Harley. "The Ghost is heading up Shore Road—wait, now he's on Main Street." They chased him and he disappeared into thin air. His Harley was white, which added to the legend. He was small and broad and had a beard, at least for the whole time that I've been alive. As he grew older his beard turned white. His hair was always a little longer than it should be and his smile always conveyed mischief. He used to tell us that we were all blessed with a full head of hair to hide our horns. He had a great wit and, despite never graduating from high school, was quick with numbers and had great commercial instincts.

His management style was fairly laissez-faire. I was always impressed with the number of newspapers he read every morning, and I took that habit with me into adulthood.

When I think of how much my formal education cost, I realize now that educations can come in all shapes and sizes and places. My cousins and I all pretty much got paid in minimum-wage cash and unlimited deli food. More valuably, we got a free education. The lessons were on dealing with people and with the government (through the Department of Motor Vehicles), selling, customer service, and being quick on your feet and clever under pressure. We were all very young, but Uncle Sal didn't care; he gave my cousin Augie the parts department, my cousin Sonny the repair and mechanics department, Bobby drove a truck, and I handled the mopeds and the helmets. I also learned about how people make decisions and how to trust my own instincts to get out of sticky situations.

We all grow up at different times and stages of life. It all depends on how we are raised. If I walked out of my house as a kid and made a left I could head over to the elementary school, or if I walked straight up the hill I could head to Ghost. Ghost was an age accelerator. There wasn't any separation of adult talk and child talk; there was just street talk, and lots of it. When *Iron Horse* magazine showed up with the Hell's Angels models, we all laughed and giggled. Maybe my friends' parents were right in their counsel to stay away. Yet one of the many things that Ghost did for me was to prepare me for adulthood and life as an entrepreneur.

If you are forced at the age of 13 to make adult decisions, these decisions become less and less stressful over time. Uncle Sal was all about baptism by fire, and he put us all through it equally. He was also unbiased by racial or other prejudices and taught us to treat all people the same despite their genetic makeup. Theodore Griffin, whom we called "Griff," was an African-American kid who grew up in our town, fought in the Vietnam War, and worked loyally for my uncle for over 35 years. When others were concerned about racial tensions in the 1960s and

1970s, my uncle used to boast that he ran Ghost like the League of Nations. He pushed us in so many ways—work ethic, creativity, time management, commercial instincts, merchandising—and he would often try to scare us to death.

■ ■ ■

It was the winter of 1981 when I turned 17 and got my driver's license. I had been practicing driving in a 1972 three-speed Dodge commercial van. We were a family surrounded with various motor vehicles so all of us had figured out how to drive by 15, but now I could legitimately make motorcycle deliveries for Uncle Sal around the tri-state area. It looked like more fun than just working around the shop and selling helmets and locks to new riders.

It was 9 P.M. on January 9, 1981. It was a freezing Friday night when Uncle Sal asked me to make a delivery.

To Harlem.

In 1981.

I was 17.

Now, take a moment and remember 1981. New York was still the crime capital of America. Times Square had not a trace of Disney. And gentrification was just another word in the dictionary. The Bronx and Harlem in the late 1970s and early 1980s were bad areas—they were considered to be part of urban blight. The blackouts and looting and general lawlessness had taken its toll on the city. In 1977, Howard Cosell said on national TV, "Ladies and gentlemen, the Bronx is burning." On August 5, 1980, Ronald Reagan visited the South Bronx at the corner of Charlotte Street and Boston Road. He was campaigning for the Presidency and he was sending a message to these areas that they weren't forgotten and they could be made better. Yet the Bronx and Harlem in 1981 were still in great disrepair and despair.

None of that mattered to Uncle Sal. I had just turned 17 and it was time for my rite of passage.

"So Uncle Sal, how do I get to 130th and Park Avenue?"

"Take the Midtown Tunnel, turn right on Park, and start counting."

Okay, that sounded easy. I strapped the bike into the back of the van and hopped in the truck. As I pulled away from the shop, though, he came out of the store like he was shot from a cannon, arms waving to get my attention. I hit the brakes.

"Are you crazy? You can't go there without the dog." He yanked open the passenger-side door and in jumped Chico, the shop's Doberman. About 90 minutes later, with Chico riding shotgun, I arrived at my destination.

On a Friday night.

In Harlem.

In 1981.

Chico and I weren't in Kansas anymore. The neighborhood was a landscape of empty buildings, some burned out, and people were gathered in groups big enough to be gangs, or to work as effectively. I stopped on the corner of 130th and Park, not knowing how I was going to find this guy. There were no BlackBerrys or cell phones back then, and even if there were, I certainly wouldn't have had one. I pulled up, put the truck in park, and waited. On a small ripped-out page of notepad I had the name of the person I was waiting for and his phone number. I was to wait there at the corner for 15 minutes and then start searching for a pay phone. Great. A few guys approached, knocked on my window and asked, "What you got in that truck?"

My adrenaline surged and my heart raced, but I now knew why it was important to bring my canine sidekick. I rolled the window down, grabbed Chico by his choker collar and shoved his face out the window. "Here's what I got in the truck." Chico's mouth was foaming, he was snarling and as I opened the van door my new friends took a few steps back. I asked if any of them knew the guy I was looking for. They knew him. Imagine that! "Well," I said bravely, "he has ten minutes to show up and pick up his bike. If not, I'm out of here."

It didn't take him more than five minutes to find out and show up.

But there was a problem. "I only got $369," he said.

Now, my uncle had told me to collect $400. I knew him well; he would go crazy if I came back with less. I was making $3 an hour and the difference was more than a day's pay.

No deal for my new friend.

I told him, "I'll give you 15 minutes to find $31, if you can't, I am gone and so is the bike." I was very scared but trying to come across like a tough guy. Chico seemed tense and was no longer foaming at my new buddies.

The guy could see how serious I was. There would be no negotiation—he sort of figured out that the discount he wanted was going to come out of my paycheck, and there was no way I was letting that happen. Roughly 14 minutes later he was back, with a brown paper bag. He emptied the contents—nickels, dimes, and quarters—onto the floor of the back of the van. We counted out $31 dollars and I gave him the bike (and to this day I wonder what soda machine the guy had broken into).

The whole time I was quaking, but I knew if I remained calm, acted tough, and kept Chico close, things were going to work out. I arrived back at the shop after midnight—and proceeded to curse out my Uncle.

He just laughed himself silly. He told me that he did that to every one of his sons and nephews; it was his 17th birthday present to us. An evening sojourn to Harlem was a fast way to learn about yourself and to learn about others. The place I visited then has totally changed for the better, which is proof that there is always hope and opportunity for human improvement. But on that night, I realized we all need to find our cool under pressure and not to be overly judgmental of others. Things often work out in unexpected ways. A couple of experiences dealing in uncertainty and a lack of shelter or security and you can greatly build up your self-confidence.

■■■

We don't have many rites of passage anymore. There are graduations and some sacraments, but our mettle doesn't get tested by tribal elders. That's unfortunate, because we inherently want to prove ourselves to people older and wiser than us, but more so, we want to prove ourselves to ourselves.

The media has fed into all of our fears. There have been too many abductions, too many missing children, and in general there is a movement among parents to hermetically seal their children away from any and all hostile elements, including germs. Think about it: We sanitize our hands constantly. Theories for the rise in allergic reactions to food include the "hygienic hypothesis," where oversanitization of the environment has led to immune system insufficiency in children.

It is hard to explain to kids today, but we all had an unstructured environment growing up. There were no Amber alerts and parents thought nothing of dropping their kids early at the elementary school so we could play football, baseball, or whatever other sport we could gin up. It was great fun and a very different world.

Now, I am all for protection, but there also needs to be the opportunity to take wing and to develop the skills of self-determination and self-reliance. At Ghost we were inoculated and given real-world vaccines. We never got an allergic reaction from bumps and scrapes from which we are now attempting to spare our children. It's a tough world out there. Learning about it early makes people more prepared for it. Also, experiencing the rough-and-tumble world has the effect of lowering people's expectations and their feeling toward entitlements. Getting the shaft or being forced to accept twists and turns prepares you to be more accepting of life's uncertainties because the truth of the matter is that no matter how hard we try, the world we live in is still not controllable.

■ ■ ■

Some of the things we learned at Ghost, we took with us to try to make our lives better; and some of the things we learned, we left behind.

My uncle was a real character, and one of his greatest skills was attracting people to that shop from all walks of life. Some of his methods weren't orthodox. We did a fair amount of advertising at Ghost in the local classifieds and in a newspaper called the *Buy-lines*. This was way before the Internet, and we made sure that every week we listed the specials and super deals to lure customers in.

I can remember a listing for a mint-condition 1975 Norton Commando that in the ad said "call for the price." When people called the next day, my Uncle implored his unorthodox sales methods.

"Come down, bring cash and make a deal."

"But Sal, what is the price?"

"I'd rather not say, just come."

"Can you give me a ballpark price?"

"Okay, you want a ball park price, $2,000."

The trouble was the bike was clearly worth $3,900.

"Two thousand? I will be right there."

And the buyer would come down to the shop ready to buy. When he got to the shop my uncle would say: "Oh, *that* bike—it's $4,150."

"What? You said the ballpark price was $2,000. What the hell happened?"

Well, if you remember from the beginning of the chapter, the shop was located next to a ballpark. My uncle would go to his desk in the front of the store, and on a piece of paper he would write in pencil "$2,000." He would turn to the customer and say, "Step outside . . . You see over that fence? That's the ballpark." He would then crumble up the piece of paper and throw it over the fence onto the ball field. "There is the price in the ballpark, but the price here in the shop is $4,150."

As kids, my cousins and I thought this tactic was hysterical, but it was also incredibly and ridiculously effective—the bike sold for $3,900. It wasn't something that I ever tried on Wall Street or in any other place in my life. It was old school. It was a technique that would have been a personal foul even in movies like *Tin Men* or *Glengarry*

Glen Ross. Again, I didn't say that I wanted to replicate everything that happened at Ghost, but I learned from most everything in that shop.

■ ■ ■

I can still hear my Uncle Sal when I told him I'd been accepted into Harvard Law School: "There is no better education than the one you got at Ghost." In a lot of ways he was right. I learned more about people and human nature there than any other place. In a retail environment, you are right at the surface membrane of all sorts of human emotions. You get the whole blend of nasty and nice. Working in a retail store helps you develop the right response skills. Ghost had it all. Tufts and Harvard— sure, they provide an education, but it was at Ghost that I *learned*.

That I eventually excelled at sales and dealing with clients, as opposed to doing mergers or trading, probably isn't a surprise considering some of my early lessons on business. During the summer of 1977, we were selling mopeds like crazy on Long Island.

My uncle saw an opportunity in the fad. His goal was to make okay but not quite great money from the moped; we sold those at a steep discount to list price. To his sons and nephews he gave the job of selling accessories. Moped kryptonite locks, mirrors, bungee cords, gas cans, and helmets—the classic high-margin stuff.

The helmet sales effort would've brought a tear to the eye of the most hardened Wall Street sales boss. We had a display with prices ranging from $10 to $150. Invariably the customer would say, "I'll take the ten-dollar helmet." My uncle taught us one response to that: "If you have a ten-dollar head you should buy a ten-dollar helmet, but when your head hits the pavement, God forbid, you are going to wish you had the $150 one." We always had the $10 ones in stock.

■ ■ ■

We learn in so many different ways from so many different experiences. Our life experience, the people we meet, the books we read, the places we travel to, the labs we experiment in all teach valuable life lessons and enhance a person's skill set. At Ghost, I acquired a knowledge base from interacting with a broad range of people and from being held accountable for my decisions. Being a financier isn't very different from being a motorcycle shop worker; the lessons learned at Ghost have worked for me among CEOs and tycoons across the globe.

So much of life just happens to us and we have to make an adjustment, yet one thing that we clearly have control over is the assimilation of knowledge. I now make my living managing relationships. All of this has been made easier by my education—the one I received at Ghost, the one for which I earned fancy degrees, and the one which I continue every day through reading and talking to people who are smarter than me or more knowledgeable.

For instance, at Ghost I learned that I always had to be on guard. Life is tough; people are difficult and oftentimes aren't fair. We need to listen well, have empathy, but also be prepared for the person who is packing a devious agenda.

Once I arrived to work on Wall Street, it became clear to me that I was fully prepared to deal with a whole plethora of personalities. I had dealt with most of these archetypes before and so I was less intimidated than some. My optimism and newness had some hard-core cynicism blended in so I was ready for the eyeball rippers. Yes, there are people on Wall Street who want to rip your eyeballs out. You need to be ready for them. The trick is to be one step ahead of them. The mistake that I have sometimes made is that I have befriended a few eyeball rippers and thought they were actually my friends. You can never let your guard down with those types of people. When I have, I have always been bitterly disappointed. Not so much with them but with myself. I know better.

One of my favorite movie scenes comes from *Saving Private Ryan*, when a German POW persuades Tom Hanks' character that he should be freed. Hanks' character releases him. During the last scene of the movie, Hanks' character is shot and killed by the very same German. He manipulated his captor and ultimately ended his young life.

Similarly, in the original *Wall Street* movie, the impatient and ambitious Bud Fox is awestruck by the fast-talking billionaire Gordon Gekko and sees him as his ticket to high life in the big city. Although Gekko appears to take Bud under his wing, he is merely using him to gather inside information about particular companies, including the airline company where his father works. When Bud eventually realizes that Gekko is trying to liquidate Bluestar Airlines, resulting in the unemployment of his father and friends, he plots for Gekko's British nemesis to buy the company. Sure, in the happily ever after world of cinema, this story had a happy ending: Buddy saved the Bluestar Airline company, his father kept his job at the company, and Gekko went to jail. In real life, things don't always work this way.

Let this be a lesson: It's okay to try to please your boss and be nice to your colleagues, but be on guard for individual and personal agendas. Sometimes someone will take an interest in helping you, in hopes to use you to get information and help themselves, as Gekko did to Buddy. Other times, people will try to get under your skin in the hope that you will leave the company. Rise above these actions. There is a rational and professional way to handle these sorts of things.

Preparing ourselves for the bad guys is only part of it. At Ghost, I learned that people must also prepare themselves for the time when they need to pounce on success. I think some of us come into life with certain predispositions. I am not saying those qualities come with us from previous lives. Some people are just luckily born with innate special gifts or are brave enough to fit their own personalities into the world around them. Think about how many great scientists may be fixing air conditioners because they made a few different decisions than the people who actually did become doctors. There are untapped geniuses out there. Through luck, timing, and circumstance they never broke through the barriers. Don't let this happen to you. Be prepared. It is a combination of reading, listening, and experiencing various challenges. It requires the habits of preparation and the work discipline that starts with the word *tireless*. Nurture these sorts of habits and your knowledge will expand exponentially.

Sometimes we nurture ourselves and sometimes other people nurture us. Our genes have laid the groundwork and design for a lot of what we have in terms of physical attributes, and science tells us that a lot of our personality comes from this as well. However, through our own free will, we can make substantial changes. It just requires the creation of good habits.

■■■

The fastest way to gain the most concentrated and highest dose of knowledge is through reading. Reading is a wonderful way to escape reality or learn something new. Fiction writers can give us great insight into the human condition by drawing parallels and relevant context into their work. Nonfiction writers, of course, can give us a great historical perspective and a base of knowledge related to so many different subjects. When I think about the hard work and the countless hours that go into the development of a book, I am reminded of the value that a person can derive from all the condensed knowledge.

From as far back as I can remember, opening up a book lit a fire of intellectual curiosity within me. In the first grade, I read 50 books (okay, so they had mostly pictures with ditties about Dick and Jane sprinkled in), and when I got to the principal's office in the spring of 1971 to pick up my ribbon I couldn't have been prouder.

My parents, while loving people, didn't really have a love of books. In fact, we didn't have very many in our house. My dad had the *Daily News* and *Newsday* delivered every day and he subscribed to *Reader's Digest* and *Time*. Other than that, it wasn't a literary home. Love? Yes. Literature? Not so much.

I still remember in 1972 when my folks opened the door for the encyclopedia salesman and he sold them the deluxe edition of the World Book, including the atlas and the dictionary. I set out with the goal to read each and every volume cover to cover. It never happened, but those books certainly helped me with my school reports.

Some of the first books I remember reading were about GI Joe and Major Matt Mason. Astronauts were cool when I was just learning how to read, so I was constantly absorbing information related to space exploration. Then came Encyclopedia Brown, the teenage detective. Every morning before school I ate several bowls of cereal and read the *Daily News* sports section. Once I got into the fifth grade, I read the Peter Benchley book *Jaws* and thought it was fantastic, though it stunted any interest I had in ocean swimming.

Although there weren't a ton of books in my house growing up, a big percentage of my educational, professional, and even personal success can be attributed to reading so many different publications and books —from Homer to Hemingway, from the *Daily News* to the *New York Times*, from *Sports Illustrated* to *Forbes*. What helped me here is maybe less that I was born with a great love of reading and more that I had the drive to do it even though no one else close to me did. I reveled in talking to other people about things I had just read, asking questions, digging deeper, and trying to find out their perspective on things. I was also interested in learning what my peers and influential role models were reading so that I, too, could read those publications. I figured if it had an impact on them it was probably worthwhile reading for me. Not only did this help me forge relationships, but it also allowed me to learn new things and challenge my original thoughts. What a nerdy admission.

Today, I still have a love for reading and I try to share this love with everyone. One of Mark Twain's most famous quotes: "The man who doesn't read good books has no advantage over the man who can't read them." We are in an age of time deficits and short attention spans. Our lives can be filled with Tweeting, texting, e-mailing, gaming, and updating our Facebook pages. All of these distractions can take away from our ability and/or our desire to read. We need to force the habit of reading into our everyday lives. By doing so, I guarantee that you will continue to expand your knowledge base. Not only will reading enrich your life, but the knowledge you learn will come in handy when you least expect it. Trust me.

■ ■ ■

Read any Greek or Roman classic and you'll learn of people who became quite powerful and then—through greed, arrogance, or hubris—took a mighty fall. Substitute certain names and places and I'd bet these stories sound just like the 2008 financial crisis. No, not exactly a Nostradamus prophecy, but a historical allegory about people who think they have found all of the answers. Taken in by their own personal smugness, they start doing things that no longer make sense. They go forward blindly, driven by their own convictions, never expecting the catastrophe that lies ahead.

Although a reading of the past cannot prepare us for everything, it can give people a sense of the human condition, historical cycles, and how to handle certain situations. Now, I'm not saying that all you have to do is read some classics, or nonfiction history books, to gain a clairvoyant knowledge of the future. But why not read about how other generations have dealt with these sorts of things? Why not learn from historical precedence and experiences?

I'm not foolish enough to believe that reading is the perfect solution to avoiding and solving particular problems. No matter how much we read, real life is still going to be different from a textbook or an ancient tablet. Just ask Fed Chairman Ben Bernanke, the well-educated expert on the Great Depression. At Milton Friedman's 90th birthday, Bernanke lauded the Nobel Prize–winning economist by saying, "Let me end my talk by abusing slightly my status as an official representative of the Federal Reserve. I would like to say to Milton and

Anna: Regarding the Great Depression. You're right. We did it. We are very sorry. But thanks to you, we won't do it again."

Now that tribute was said in November 2002 in the halcyon era of steady Goldilocks low-inflation growth. At that time the Fed and others thought they had it all figured out. In August 2007, Fed Chairman Bernanke said in congressional testimony that he thought the subprime problem was limited to about $95 billion of exposure. There is a big difference between $95 billion and the $6 trillion that the Fed and the U.S. government created to help bring the crisis to an end.

It is often said that history doesn't repeat itself but often rhymes. As you may know, there are few people on the planet as knowledgeable about the Great Depression as our esteemed Fed chairman. Yet he didn't see the financial crisis of 2008 coming. Although he had probably read a million publications about the Great Depression, he was in uncharted territory just like the rest of us.

We must be on guard for the unknowable. We must remember that we are never fully prepared for all of modern life's surprises. But if we have our knowledge and wits about us, we can overcome any obstacle and oftentimes emerge bigger and better than before.

■ ■ ■

Knowledge is also acquired in the home. From a young age, our parents teach us the basic concept of knowing right from wrong.

During my childhood, I gained an understanding that some rules—the ones made by the people in charge—need to be followed. My parents may not have always understood what I was doing or why I was doing it, but they always made sure I was doing it the right way.

In my case, the person in charge was my father. He expected us to do two things: work and do well in school. My mom took care of my grandfather and made sure our beds were made and our bellies fed. She was committed to loving us and had mastered the distribution of Catholic guilt to the point that the Pope should give her an honorary degree.

In kindergarten, I stole a pair of plastic handcuffs. To this day I still can't recall why or from whom, but my mom knew they weren't mine. When she challenged me, I protested that someone gave them to me. She said I was lying and was heading straight to hell when I died to be tortured by the devil himself. He would burn me and for an eternity stab me with his pitchfork. When these intimidating tactics didn't pull a confession out of me, she mandated that we march right up to church so that I could tell the priest the truth.

Petrified, I swallowed hard and spilled the beans. It never, ever happened again. I can still feel the chill in my stomach. At my first confession, before my first communion, I explained the whole thing to the priest behind the veiled screen. He was holding back laughter, but I could sense his smile as he proceeded to hand down a half-dozen Hail Mary's and an Our Father. That was it. God forgave me and I was spared the devil's pitchfork. No wonder Christianity caught on.

The neighborhood I lived in was loaded with several of my cousins and children my age. There were no play dates, just unscheduled activities. We went up to the local school and played for hours. The only rule to which we needed to adhere to was to be home by 5:30. That was dinnertime, and enforcement could be extreme. My brother and I learned that on a day my dad had tickets to a Nets playoff game, back when they played at the Nassau Coliseum. We erroneously thought we could get home at 6 because we were going to eat at the game. Wrong. We walked into the house, and my Dad took the tickets off the kitchen counter and ripped them up in front of our eyes.

When I remember that day, I often think about the generation that I live in today and how indulgent we are as parents. There is no way I or any of my contemporaries would do that to today's children. We are pliable. It is an interesting social experiment. In our effort to build self-esteem and to make our children feel good about themselves, we have made everything easy.

What are they learning?

That the world will always bend to them? Sadly, that won't be the case, and the worst part is that they won't learn that lesson from the people who love them most in the world.

In 1810, children were to be seen and not heard, didn't speak until spoken to, and were sent out into the fields to work as soon as they were able to. The high child mortality rate meant that there were a lot of kids and that many died before they reached adulthood. The child's place as servant and helper to the family was strictly enforced—in fact, for most people, economic survival demanded it.

In 2010, we are slaves to our kids. In 1810, children used a shovel, a pitchfork, an ax, and possibly a washboard. In 2010, they use an iPhone, an iPod, an iPad, a laptop, a YouTube account, and unlimited Legos, and they go to Miley Cyrus and Jonas Brothers concerts.

In the 1970s, we had it easy but there was discipline and at times the belt. It will be interesting to see how the current generation of children eventually parent. Perhaps they will mirror my generation or come up with a new strategy. My theory is that the people of my generation remember thinking to themselves that when I have my kids I am going to go the extra mile and do things for them that weren't done for me. Go to every soccer game, be at every school sing-along, buy them stuff that we felt deprived of. So this has now been done to a generation en masse. Perhaps when our kids grow up they will think that they had it easy and unstructured, so they had better impose more discipline on their kids. It will be interesting to see how it all turns out.

When I was growing up, one of the best lines that my dad used was, "God chose me to be your parent, not your friend." Today parents are friends first, parents later. Maybe the discipline we got as kids made us weak and fearful of conflict with our kids. I don't know the reason, but I do think it will be interesting to see how this new generation applies the life lessons they learned to their future generation.

■■■

You can also learn a lot from all different types of people—young and old, rich or poor. One of my colleagues at Goldman, a Harvard Business School graduate by the name of Greg Hoogkamp, said something to me that I never forgot. His father was a detective on an upstate New York police force. He taught his son a very important lesson: Never underestimate the intelligence of anybody. You really never know who you are talking to, what their level of life experience is, or what you can learn from them. You can be easily fooled if you start slotting people into easy stereotypes or if, because of their youth, you assume that you might have an edge.

For instance, there was a young man in the 1980s who was a sophomore at the University of Texas and he said he was going to compete with IBM. People scoffed. His name was Michael Dell. There was another young man who was a sophomore at Harvard in 1990 and he had aspirations to rise up and become one of the top money managers of his generation. His name was Ken Griffin. I sometimes think of the people who met these guys as youngsters and thought that their ideas were silly, and I wince. Take no one for granted. Intelligence and learning come in many varieties. A British or Brooklyn accent? Don't overly judge—smarts and dumbness come in a lot of varieties. Proceed with caution.

■ ■ ■

It is often said that lessons come from unlikely places and the most unlikely times . . . and the spring of 1982 proved no exception.

March 1982 was an exciting time for me. I was about to hear from school and I was thrilled that soon I would be going to college. The critical thing for me to do was to save money, so I was working 40 hours a week at the motorcycle shop—that would take the whole weekend and several days a week after school. One afternoon a man entered the shop and asked to see a mechanic. He was slight, about 5′8″ tall, and had a full beard. At first glance, I thought I knew him but couldn't place his face. I brought his beautiful new Harley to the service area.

When my cousin Augie returned from a delivery, he was very excited. "Anthony, Billy Joel is in the store."

"Come on. Are you kidding? Where?"

"That's him, right there."

"Really?" Wow. He was about as low-key as anyone I had waited on. He was unpretentious and regular. It was my first interaction with a celebrity and I was starstruck. I was impressed with his demeanor. I didn't want to bother him but I couldn't wait to tell my friends.

"How much longer?" Billy asked me.

"I just want to tell you how much I love your work."

"Thanks. When do you think they will get done replacing my chain?"

"Maybe another 20 minutes."

"Okay, sounds good. I am starving. Is there a place around here where I can get some pizza?"

"Yes, I can drive you there."

Now, I was totally pumped. I was taking Billy Joel, the king of Long Island rock and roll, to Carlo's Pizzeria in my 1979 burgundy Camaro, replete with a Pioneer power booster. When we got to Carlo's, everyone—and I mean everyone—recognized the Piano Man. And what did he do? He signed autographs, took questions, allowed a few teenage girls a chance to get their cameras and take pictures, and he was an all-around nice guy.

On the way back, he explained why he didn't just get his pizza and run. He told me about his burning desire to be a musician and his anxiety about whether he'd succeed. He said his success was about more than talent; it was about luck and timing.

Then he added the most important point. "I made one promise to myself though: If it came to pass, I wouldn't let it ruin my relationships with strangers. After all, the fans are the ones that have made me."

It was about the classiest thing I had heard up until that time. It was his understanding of human life and pathos that made him so great.

He wasn't a philosopher or a Greek scholar. He was a rock-and-roll singer. But he learned how to deal with people; how to touch them and manifest their joy and pain—from Vietnam veterans to steelworkers, fisherman, even uptown girls. It may not be the classic genius, but more people can't do it than can. To me, that's a smart man, and from him I learned the importance of treating all people with kindness and not acting overly self-important.

There is a big difference between street smarts and book smarts. However, there's not much difference in terms of the way they are acquired. They may show up in different places but the same things are required: curiosity, concentration, and the ability to figure out how and why things work. It could be a carburetor or a CAT scan. The skills are different, but what you do to develop them is pretty much the same.

We gain knowledge from many sources. We gain wisdom from few. If I could offer one suggestion on how to *attain* wisdom, I would simply say: Be on the lookout, as you can learn it from everybody and anybody. Pay attention.

Further, on the street where I grew up, if it sounds too good to be true, it probably is. Knowledge, wisdom, common sense—these are all works in progress. We learned some hard lessons about a lot of things in 2008. Here's the only one you need to remember on *retaining* knowledge: Keep learning, because you don't know everything.

Chapter 6

The Way of the Mentor
Looking for a Hero

An educated consumer is our best customer.

—*Sy Syms*

Okay, so I shopped at Syms.

Syms was famous in New York. In 1989, it had a warehouse-style store in Lower Manhattan. According to its founders, Sy and Marcy Syms, it sold "designer name" suits at discount prices. I bought suits there for $199 and ties for $7. It was mostly stuff from a few seasons ago or some slightly irregular inventory where a stitch was slightly off or a button was loose. And the designer names were ones you probably hadn't heard of or, more precisely, sounded something like one you had heard of.

Being the educated consumer that I was, I bought some dress shirts with a healthy amount of polyester in them—60/40 cotton/poly blended shirts to be exact. No ironing required, they came right out of the dryer and could be put on the hanger, good to go. I paired this load of poly with thin black ties and pointy shoes. In 1989, I brought my fashion sense with me to Goldman Sachs. I figured the clothes were cheaper, didn't wrinkle much, and hey, who'd know the difference?

Mike Fascitelli, who was one of the heads of Goldman's Real Estate Finance unit, did and actually got in my face about it. "Mooch, the shirts and ties have to go. Go out and get some real clothes," he said one day. "You need to look a bit more professional."

I was embarrassed. But I took his advice, went to the Custom Shop and bought some shirts, ties, and a suit. My credit card balance got higher but so did the quality of my presentation to the outside world. Knowing that I didn't have enough money to buy an entire new wardrobe, Mike then did the most gracious thing ever: He gave me two suits and a tux. I still have the tux.

When I started making a little dough, Mike and his wife Beth took me shopping at Barney's clothing warehouse in New Jersey. Mike had access to the wholesale warehouse because Barney's was one of his clients and he offered to bring me. Together we bought designer suits, shirts, and ties for 40 percent off retail. More importantly, we talked about business and life.

Mike's advice was direct, smart, and spot-on. He was trying to help a young man better understand his new position in life. He was becoming my mentor. That was 1989.

In 1992, Mike made partner at Goldman. He should have made it in 1990 but they tested his temperance, patience, and perseverance and made him wait. Like me, he didn't entirely fit in; he was just a little bit too charismatic and too magnetic. Great with numbers, human beings, wine, golf, hoops, he had a great intellectual capacity but liked being "regular" and one of the guys. No air of superiority, he knew where he was going and he was determined to be nice to people the whole way. According to his alma mater's alumni publication, he attributed his success to "being in the right place at the right time, having the right mentors, and getting a few lucky breaks. Also, being humble, not being arrogant, and treating all people with respect. And I am not a bad negotiator."

Still, nothing was handed to him.

Mike was from Rhode Island, grew up in a working-class Italian-American family, went to the University of Rhode Island, and graduated from Harvard Business School. The neighborhood he grew up in was sort of like the neighborhood I'm from on Long Island, if not a touch worse. He was the first in his family to attend college; his father was a tailor, his mother was a seamstress, and his older brother built and renovated houses. Although Mike wasn't initiated in the ways of business, his role models at home embodied a work ethic that kept him grounded and gave him street smarts.

In a lot of ways, Mike's modest background was similar to mine—complete with the loud Sundays dinners and plastic on the furniture. Although unifying, these common experiences and shared bonds wouldn't have been enough for the mentoring relationship that we eventually developed. Mike became my mentor because I was lucky enough that our paths crossed at Goldman. Almost instantly, our personalities clicked and we got along really well as we had similar values and goals. But what made it last was that Mike took an interest in my professional and personal growth and took the time to steer me in the right direction. He is a genuine guy and I'm lucky that I met him.

As my mentor, Mike never told me what he thought I wanted to hear. He was raw and I could always count on him to tell me the truth. If I didn't like what he was saying, too bad. One thing though: It was honest, so a failure to listen and potentially heed would be done at my own peril.

I have made my share of mistakes in my career. I never felt that Mike judged me, even in my worst moments. I always knew that he wanted me to rise to the top.

Over the years, I have learned a lot from Mike. I've learned the importance of dressing for success. I've learned that I should always have a three- to five-year career plan but to be flexible since we can't predict the future. I've learned to pick myself up, face failure head-on, and move on to something better. I've learned how to be a good mentor. Perhaps most importantly, I learned that I needed to find my passion, pursue it, and never lose my authenticity.

Today, Mike is CEO of Vornado Realty Trust, a real estate investment trust with a $10 billion market capitalization and a portfolio of more than 100 buildings in America's biggest cities. We still laugh about my wardrobe deficiency and how he set me straight. More importantly, he still talks to me about my career and life and offers raw and honest advice. It's a good feeling to have that sort of person in your life, and you should try to be that sort of person for someone else.

■■■

I encourage all people, especially young people, to have a Mike in their lives, a trustworthy mentor. Despite the arrogance of youth and a person's self-perceived omniscience, most people are generally quite clueless about how to advance at work and respond to corporate life. A mentor can help you navigate the waters and provide valuable career and personal advice.

We need people in our lives who openly share their stories with us and offer perspective and guidance. Their words of wisdom are a voice that you'll be forced to listen to and hear, even if your mentor is saying something painful. You'll be drawn to it, almost thirsty for knowledge and trying like hell to do the things that you in turn believe will make your mentor proud. With this impulse will come a need to make sure your mentor knows that you are coachable and working hard to set and then reach your goals.

No matter your age, you need to surround yourself with people who will give you advice and viewpoints that vary from your own. People often get blindsided when they don't have all the answers but think they do. Don't let this happen to you. Seek out a mentor who will give you a hard run around the thought track and who will challenge your assumptions—one who will take the time to get to know you, your interests, your passions, your skills.

Where do you find such a mentor? Having the right mentor sometimes is a matter of luck, as was the case with Mike and me. I was very fortunate to get my career started at Goldman, a place full of exceptionally smart people, some of whom were actually looking out for me.

John McNulty, David Darst, Bob Castrignano, and Bill Gruver were all part of my personal board of directors. These men all had very different personalities, but all genuine in their interest in helping me. And they all helped me in different ways.

As you know from Chapter 2, Mike got me a job in an area that matched my skill set and young career ambitions. Sure, he first had to fire me, but he also helped me get rehired.

Mike also taught me about the importance of dressing for success. In business, you have to look a certain part. The clothes don't make the man, but they add confidence and send the right signal about your personal style. As a kid, I remember thinking: What's the big deal? But it is a big deal. Your appearance makes a first impression on people; none of us actually like this, but we are judged within a few minutes. If you don't look the part, especially in business, you'll give the wrong impression to prospects, bosses, and clients.

Perhaps the most important thing that I learned from Mike that I pass on to you and to my mentors is this: Don't lose your authenticity. Be comfortable with the many facets that make up your personality. Why change or morph what you have? There is no price tag you can put on your own personality to make it worth exchanging it for conformity.

For all of its greatness, Goldman did that to a lot of people. The firm did a remarkable job of attracting, training, and retaining some of the best talent, but they encouraged a culture of conformity, and frowned upon certain personality traits. This isn't a bad thing and it has led to their success, but it also has caused many good workers to find their way out of the system—they either were weeded out or went to a firm where they could be themselves.

Trying hard to be someone you're not is exhausting. John Kennedy once said of Richard Nixon: "I feel sorry for Nixon . . . at each stop he has to decide which Nixon he is at the moment, which must be very exhausting." For instance, I am confident that one of my friends and former colleagues hated every minute of his life at Goldman but he stayed there because he loved the accompanying money and status.

How exhausting—that person is 45 but looks 60. Don't let this happen to you. On the other hand, I am confident that one of my former Harvard Law classmates never changed one iota of his personality as he rode up the corporate ladder and eventually became partner at Goldman. He always stayed true to himself and exerted patience and discipline.

Over the course of 20 years on Wall Street, I have experienced all kinds of twists and turns. I have experienced the exhilaration of success and profits, the pain of failure, the pangs of fear, and the temptation of greed. Yet I am proud to say that I have always stuck with who I am. The temptation for the trappings of wealth and status is nothing short of a financial black hole. It sucks you in. I don't look down on it; heck, I was a part of it. I just urge you to look at it critically and know what you are signing up for. And if you realize that you hate your job, be brave enough to leave it even if your peers covet it and it pays you the big bucks.

Remember, the best version of you is the way you define yourself when you are daydreaming—when your self-consciousness is low and your self-awareness is high; when it dawns on you that this is your life and it's a pretty good one; when the bellyaching and whining stop; when you are proud to say who you are.

Mentors, at least the right ones, will be honest with you and will help in finding this version of you.

■ ■ ■

As I mentioned previously, I was fortunate enough to have multiple mentors. Mentors can help you in a lot of ways.

Mentors can help you face the music by giving you a dose of honest advice—and there's nothing like brutal honesty to wake you up in the morning. A former submariner and Navy man, Bill Gruver was perhaps the toughest partner at Goldman Sachs. Most of my young, inexperienced colleagues avoided him because he would pick apart their psyches and criticize their work. Yet there was a small group of us who sought him out. When he retired in 1992, I would travel to Eaglesmere, Pennsylvania, to visit him and talk openly about my career track at Goldman. One day, while we were walking in the woods, I complained to him. At the time, I felt my managers were discrediting the intensity of my work effort and weren't providing me with enough feedback. He stopped walking, looked me straight in the face, and said, "Stop whining and pick yourself up." It was a cold slap in the face and the hits just kept on coming. He continued, "Buck up. You're not that important yet. Deal with it. And stop complaining." I needed that slap; it caused me to act more positively.

Mentors can help you answer questions that you are unsure about. And the good ones don't just mentor you in the office—they can often teach you a lot about life. For instance, one day David Darst and I took an early flight to Boston. We were in town to recruit at Harvard. Being one of the most entertaining and enlightened guys in the industry, we took a slight detour and visited the Busch-Reisinger Museum. He had a tour guide waiting for us and we walked the halls examining the neo-Raphaelite paintings. He was a work-hard, play-hard type of guy, a true Renaissance man, or at least as close to one as you'll get on Wall Street. Through this experience he showed me the importance of balancing work with life. Get your work done and live a little—it's okay to make some time for fun stuff, especially culture.

A mentor may even be able to save your job. Bob Matza, who was president and chief operating officer of Neuberger and the person who bought our company in 2001, has offered insight into this topic and believes that there are many smart, hardworking people who never achieve the success they should because they don't have a mentor. He says, "In the sweeping management changes that have been routine on Wall Street, if you don't have a mentor you could be a casualty despite your skill level."

One word of caution: Be careful not to develop a mentoring relationship with a seemingly successful experienced person who is dishonest, disingenuous, or self-serving. Sure, they may help you make fast money but the relationship and your success won't last long. Moreover, the advice they give probably will be to your detriment. Gordon Gekko's mentorship of Bud Fox is a perfect example. Sure, Gekko taught Bud about the business, took the time to talk to him about his personal life, and even bought him a suit, but his interest was not in helping Bud's career; it was in helping himself. As a naïve puppy dog, Bud jumped through hoops to do what Gekko requested of him, including serving as a mole and participating in insider trading. And when Gekko got what he wanted from this relationship, he could have cared less about Bud's career or life. In Gekko's own words to Bud, "It's all about bucks, kid. The rest is conversation."

■■■

Funny thing about mentors, you can never do for them what they do for you. It is an asymmetric relationship. Sure, they get a kick out of helping you, but their side is pretty selfless. On some level, there is nothing that I can really do for Mike other than support him and cheer him on. The best I can do for him is write fund-raiser and charity checks, and if he asks my honest opinion about somebody or a business idea I will tell him what I think. Because of the age spread and varying experiences, however, it's almost impossible for me to have much impact.

If you are a mentee, all you can really do is pay it forward by mentoring someone else in the future. I have tried to do so throughout my career. I have even given my share of suits away. I've offered advice, tried to help people navigate the twists and turns of a career, and also once in a while said a prayer for their success and happiness.

I take great pride in trying to mentor people. At SkyBridge Capital, the firm that I helped start and am now a co-managing partner of, we try to help people grow so that they can realize their dreams and start their own asset management businesses. Mentoring is a huge part of this job, and we find it particularly important to mentor and guide our young managers.

In 2008, as the market was melting down, I sat down individually with some of the young managers whose funds we had seeded. I didn't give them any hand-me-down suits, but I sought to mentor them during this unsettling time by offering them the wisdom of my experience and some words of encouragement.

I simply and seriously laid out the facts:

> I have been here before, in 1998, and had several missteps that almost cost me my business and career. We lost clients' money and there is nothing more painful than that. The goal right now is survival. You can survive down 20 percent but you can't survive down 40 percent.

This was a little bit of an exaggeration as you can survive anything that doesn't kill you. However, I wanted to make sure these young managers understood the importance of business survival—the goal is to make it through the cycle. I wanted to help them handle the risks of being in an excessively volatile business. The 10,000-year flood happens every five years on Wall Street, no matter what the computer models or the propeller heads say. So I encouraged them to always be prepared and be defensive.

One of the people I talked to was Jonathan Urfrig. In 2006, I met Jonathan after he had left a fairly big and very well-known hedge fund, Third Point LLC, to launch his own operation, U Capital. He had $80 million under management and was doing a very good job. Although he was a smart analyst/portfolio manager, he was having a hard time raising money while also focusing on the firm's investments.

In 2006, he came to SkyBridge because he thought he could grow a more stable and diversified business with our help. We had built a reputation for putting more into something than we were taking out, and he recognized it, so it seemed like a natural fit. When Jonathan spoke, I was very impressed that he had the guts to pursue his passion, as he so badly wanted to start his own business. I believed he had the fortitude and intensity to stick things out. In 2007, SkyBridge funded him

$50 million and he gave our clients a piece of his business. When the economy started rocking in late 2007 and ultimately crashed in 2008, I gave Jonathan the survival speech. He listened intently and closed down elements of his portfolio. And he went on to have a great year, and is surviving.

In contrast, I gave another fund manager the same speech. But he could not bring himself to listen to my advice. He thought he was too smart for us. Guess what—he cratered.

His failure to listen—which consequently caused his investment to plummet—caused us to fire him. He was probably right in that he was smarter than we were, but he couldn't resist the urge to be a know-it-all. He failed to adequately respect the value of experience and recognize that it counts for something. He let inexperience and a stubborn streak cost his clients and it harmed his business.

I am not saying that my partners or I know it all or that we always dispense sage advice. Sometimes we are wrong; but we do have experience and a seasoned skill set that has allowed us to learn firsthand. We will not always be right. One of my closest friends and mentors, Frank Meyer, says when you offer a lot of advice and ideas, you have to assume that some of it will be wrong. We are far from perfect, but we try to help guide our mentees down the best possible path by helping them learn from our experiences and mistakes.

The manager who ignored my advice during the great meltdown of 2008 did so at his own peril. I lived through a Wall Street recession at Goldman in the early 1990s where some firms were simply firing people by MBA class, starting with the youngest. I survived a major crisis at Oscar Capital in 1998. When the Russian ruble became devalued, our hedge fund was set back. Through discipline and grit we recovered and we also adapted. We built a robust, separately managed account business and my partners and I put our firm in a position to be seen as a strong acquisition target by a major money management firm. That was good for my team and good for me. I survived a dot-com disaster in 2001 running a hedge fund when others crashed and burned.

Regardless, it's a shame that this young manager didn't listen to our advice. He was likeable and smart, but those qualities oftentimes are not enough.

Are you the kind of person who can take criticism? Are you capable of just hearing or also listening? What happens when things aren't going as planned? Are you rigid or adaptive? Can you ask for help, or is your ego such that you can't help yourself by asking?

What typically shuts people down are their insecurities, their fear of exposure. They think, "I need to prove to the person giving the advice how smart I am or how right I am. I will show them." And so what happens? They act out of ego or pride and then start on the path of self-destruction.

The ability to be coached, to take constructive criticism, and to adapt when circumstances call for change are all part of the necessary skills for success. Plans change; it happens to everybody. Part of being an entrepreneur is admitting mistakes and weaknesses and trying to adapt to the existing environment. Jack Welch often says, "Deal with the world the way it is, not the way you want it to be." For the young business owner this is especially true, and not adhering to this sort of advice could drive your operation into an early grave.

Self-awareness, humility, personal insight, adaptation—all of these traits require a dropping of the ego. Most people on Wall Street have healthy egos; the ones that are unhealthy are the egotists, believing in their own righteousness or invincibility. They need to prove to people that they were right at all costs and are often blinded by their relative and respective amounts of certainty. Either they stopped listening long ago or didn't have the right sort of mentors around them.

It's easy to vilify these people but we have to recognize that each of us has these sorts of weaknesses. So protect yourself. Don't let your ego prevent you from seeking out a mentor or learning from others.

And never think that you are too old or experienced to have a mentor. Mentors come in all age groups, shapes, and sizes. Surround yourself with great people who are willing to call you out and guide you from their own experience. Find people who can help you find yourself.

■ ■ ■

There are many things I love about what I do. I like raising money and meeting interesting people in the process. I like helping clients reach their goals and, as I've said before, working with other people to turn their dreams into real businesses is a joy. Of all those, I enjoy the mentoring part in a special way. There's something about giving advice—whether it be on business or on how to choose a career, college, or business school—that energizes me. It's not that I know better. It's that I naturally can tune in to people and figure out what makes them tick.

I think what makes me an effective mentor goes back to my appreciation for individuality and nonconformity. I often think that the most charismatic people get that way from just being themselves. They can lighten a room with humor, usually by saying something that is very true but that others would feel uncomfortable saying or hearing.

For instance, 10 years ago I met with a spunky, artsy kid whose dad was a hot shot on Wall Street. It was clear to me that his powerful dad was pushing a Wall Street career, while the kid dreamed of a career in Hollywood, film, and media. The dad even went so far as to tell me to tell him to work on the Street. What did I do? The complete opposite: I told the kid to go straight to Hollywood, pursue his passion, and realize his dream. Today, he is an award-winning advertiser who's very plugged in and passionate about his life and career. Now, I know the story could have had an unhappy ending, with the kid waiting tables and living out of his car (or his trust fund paying his bills), but the point I'm trying to make is that a mentor needs to understand the people he is attempting to coach.

As a mentor and co-partner, I always want the people around me to really excel. The better they do, the happier I am. But remember, SkyBridge is a business. It's not charity work. It's also a very nice intersection of what I love to do and what my partners and I think can be quite lucrative over the long haul. Essentially, the company centers on our idea that smaller managers can outperform larger ones (that's the lucrative part), and that financing the new minds can be very lucrative (that's the nurturing, hand-holding, showing-them-what-to-do part). We researched this theory for about a year and found that, quite simply, larger managers wield a bigger asset base and therefore can't be as nimble in volatile markets. They fear that doing something different or a bit risky may jeopardize their fat management fees. As a result, most large managers hug the major indexes and the conventional wisdom that goes with them.

Smaller managers have fears, too—that they won't have the time to balance raising money, managing employees, and doing the actual investing. We help solve one of those challenges by using our vast network of connections and clients to amass enough money for them to have a good base of investors beyond their friends and families. We also have a fully integrated risk management group to help them evaluate the portfolio management risk that investors are taking. But that doesn't mean that we don't offer advice on shaky employees, firms they work with, or any number of other things.

Mentoring younger people, or people who have never experienced the tumult or uncertainty of entrepreneurship, excites me and lets me perpetually pursue my passion. At SkyBridge, the business is about constant change and adaptation. We are constantly looking for new investment themes and new talent. We still live in a culture that rewards innovative thinking and fresh ideas. SkyBridge likes to be there in the asset management business.

The foundation of my beliefs on mentoring is to let young people play to their strengths, not yours; let mavericks be mavericks and shy rocket scientists be shy rocket scientists. Everyone has his own personality DNA. Don't smudge it or try to remake it in your own image. The best mentor wants his protégé to be comfortable in his own skin and be capable of expressing his full personality. Don't be the type of mentor that snuffs out individuality and forces a person to conform to a particular culture. At SkyBridge we run in smaller packs, so mavericks are okay. They help to shake things up.

Remember, your mentee is not you. Don't always give advice from the point of view of what you think you did right and wrong. Training someone or helping them to build a career requires a light touch. The younger person is heading out into the world with his own arc, his own personality, and his own struggles. Your job is to help him become the best person that he can be, not some ideal of yourself that never happened.

Talk to your mentees, give them important books and articles to read, force them into key discussions, and help them balance humility and a healthy self-confidence.

But my co-partner and I don't do this alone. We have a valuable advisory team that helps to mentor our young managers. Former NFL star Mel Blount once said everyone should be reaching for the stars with one hand and pulling someone up behind him with the other hand. This poetic thought stresses the importance of passing down the wisdom of experience to others. More importantly, it encourages people to take in other people to improve themselves. In the same way that mixed-breed dogs are thought to be sturdier and more adaptable than purebred dogs, so are organizations that can develop hybrid vigor. In other words, a company that takes in outsiders is better able to adapt to dynamic environments because of the nondismissive input from external advisers. The advisory team at SkyBridge is made up of those mixed breeds.

One of the most valuable advisory committee members at SkyBridge is Frank Meyer. Frank is famous in our industry for backing Ken Griffin, who became one of the most successful hedge fund managers of his generation. In a small dorm room at Harvard in 1988, Frank gave Ken a million dollars to help him start and develop his business. This venture ultimately became Citadel, one of the most powerful firms in finance.

Frank believes in all of the great values of life—kindness, humility, charity, self-awareness—and is perhaps one of most knowledgeable people I have ever met. Yet he isn't arrogant enough to believe he knows it all. Instead, he simply helps the mentee finds his way. He pushes more than a shrink but pulls less than a puppeteer.

■■■

You can also learn a lot from those whom you mentor. While they may be learning from you, the truth is you can also learn from them. This then becomes a domino effect because the more you learn from them, the better you can relate to their generational struggle. In turn, they will learn more from you because they'll think you can relate to them and so they can relate to you.

Most smart young people are yearning to make a difference and to prove that they have what it takes. Most old people think they are kids and have a limited ability to add value. The truth is in the middle. If you don't give new people a chance, and baptize them in fire, you are hurting your company. That's not to say you need to let a 24-year-old be the CEO, but you should do your best to give them opportunity and responsibility.

Part of who we are is related to our personal background and education, but another big part of it is generational. If you don't know how to Twitter, for instance, but read about it six times a week in the *New York Times* and see every CNN anchor talking about it, it's time to pull one of the young guns in your company in and find out about it. Then figure out a way to make it applicable to your business. They inform you and you inform them. That's the basis for a beautiful relationship.

It's not just the old fogies that you can learn from—the young sometimes teach the most, especially about where the world is going. Young people have energy and new ideas. They may see something obvious to them that you are oblivious to. Experience counts for a lot but it sometimes has a blind eye to progress. If it hasn't been done before, then chances are that you will pass on trying it. Your experience could make you rigid or against experiments. Most young people aren't that jaded yet. Thank goodness.

If you were born after 1980, chances are you have gotten very comfortable in the digital world and find it very easy to communicate with people through e-mail, text messaging, and other impersonal tools. One of the things that the younger people in my office have taught me is that their world is a more brightly colored, visual one. They love the graphics on the Internet. The younger people in my office figured out that the best way to reach people of their generation through our marketing material was to make sure our PowerPoint presentations had the look and feel of the best web sites. Many of the graphics in our material look like iPhone apps. So cool.

Apparently, you now need to be cool to communicate. I did my college application on a typewriter; today people are submitting them over the Web from a Mac. Sit down with some of the younger people in your life and ask them about the world that they are creating. Be fresh, be relevant, embrace youth. Who knows—you may be talking to the next young innovative billionaire.

Mentoring is quite rewarding, and all of us who do it know that we learn a lot from the process. The friendships that are developed and the joy of watching others succeed are also key to your building your own fortune. It just plain feels good to help others do better. Just remember, every person and every situation is different and needs to be handled delicately. And always remember to thank your own mentors.

■ ■ ■

At SkyBridge, I like asking people, young and old, how I am doing. The smart ones will tell me the truth. I'm human; I make a lot of mistakes. How are you and I going to get better if people don't offer us their honest words and opinions? Make sure you bring people into your game who can treat your head like a pencil and their brains as a sharpener. You will do yourself a disservice and all of those around you if you surround yourself with yes-people and sycophants.

I often think about Steve Roth, former CEO and current chairman of Vornado Realty. He had the confidence in 1996 to hire Mike Fascitelli. He paid him at the time an unheard-of fortune to join his senior management team. Mike is now CEO, Steve is now chairman, and there has been an incredible amount of value created for their shareholders and employees. Be brave enough to surround yourself with the smartest, and good things will happen.

Lehman didn't, and its story didn't end well.

Lehman was inbred. They were a group of survivors who pulled through some very bad moments. Each time they pulled through they became a stronger and stronger company. The trouble is it reinforced their arrogance in their decision making. Rob Kapito, the president of BlackRock, once said that he and Larry Fink (BlackRock's CEO) were worried every day that they were going to go out of business and that their name that adorned their building would be taken down. Constant fear and constant paranoia about survival are not bad things, but not doing anything about it *is* a bad thing.

At Lehman they rode a market roller coaster on heavy leverage and kept surviving, so they kept raising stakes, believing in their own invincibility. Making a huge fortune for lots of people probably didn't instill a lot of corporate self-doubt. Yet Kapito and Fink had the fear. Where does it come from? Is it training, or perhaps college education? Maybe it comes from good mentoring. I am not exactly sure where it comes from, but for me it is a product of all of those things. Who was mentoring Joe Gregory or Dick Fuld? Were they capable of listening? Or long ago did the self-assurance flaps cover up their ears, allowing only obsequious praise to filter in?

Fuld said in sworn Congressional testimony that "Until the day they put me into the ground, I will wonder . . . why we were the only ones" that were not rescued. Now perhaps some people might say not saving Lehman was unfair given that others were saved. What is troublesome about Mr. Fuld's comments is that he had to know that his and other businesses like his were imperiled. Could the lack of self-awareness be that high, or lack of self-doubt be that low? Success can reinforce security and self-confidence.

The street I grew up on and the street that both of my parents came from were fraught with uncertainty. Things can go wrong and often do. Seek out mentors who can help you prepare for this. No matter what your age, you need advice, and at times you need to heed it. One of the many lessons of the Lehman debacle is one of listening. Who were they listening to? Don't just listen to people who are saying things that you want to hear. Find your true self by having the intellectual curiosity to understand dissent.

In the summer of 2009, I got to know Oliver Stone and understand dissent. He made me a technical adviser on the sequel to *Wall Street*, which is called *Wall Street: Money Never Sleeps*. I immediately got up to speed by buying the DVDs of all of his movies and listening to his director commentaries. To many, Oliver is a controversial guy—media types, politicians, and establishment business leaders are often horrified by him. He forces them to think of the alternative viewpoint to their thinking. This typically riles people up. Yet I firmly believe that this Academy Award–winning director just wants to challenge people intellectually by asking them provocative questions and challenging their ideological viewpoints. This dissent helps us sharpen our focus and clarify our own ideas, even if it doesn't sway us from our point of view. Be the type of person who can deal with hearing the opposing point of view. Have the self-confidence and intellectual security to include people in your life who may not see everything the same way you do. It will be good for your career in the same way that it's good for society.

■■■

If you can empower yourself with open mindedness, then you will become stronger and more confident, but don't stop there; make training and improvement a constant goal for you and your company.

There can never be enough training. Training is having workshops, peer sit-downs, cutting out newspaper and magazine articles, and passing out books people should read. Everybody needs training and guidance. I always tell my new staff members to carry a notebook around with them so that they can write down questions as they come up. I remind them that no question is too stupid and no one should make you feel dumb asking a question.

Now all this training doesn't have to be squishy and huggy. The Marine Corps mentors people but it doesn't feel particularly uplifting at the time. It's not supposed to. When you're at Parris Island, you're being mentored on the best way to keep yourself and those around you alive. Goldman Sachs was similar in the way it trained people. Because of my, uh, unique experience at the firm, I was trained *twice*—once in investment banking and another time in the equities division. The difference was stark: While investment bankers were focused on teamwork, on the equities side we were trained with an ethos of teamwork but also to be client kamikazes. Our goal was to kill ourselves for the client and make them know it and feel it. How is one trained to do that?

The lesson came in what was easily the most memorable moment of my training class. It was Memorial Day weekend, 1991, and during it, I learned the big lesson that explained the golden era of Goldman Sachs.

On that Friday, the start of a holiday weekend for most civilized Americans and those who don't work in retail, 40 of us were told to report to a conference room on the 29th floor of 85 Broad Street at 5 P.M. "Well, that sucks," was the natural knee-jerk reaction. No mercy for the yuppies. By 4:59 P.M. all 40 of us were present and accounted for.

At 5, the partner who was supposed to be running the meeting hadn't shown up. No biggie. By 6, no partner. We waited. At 7, still no partner. Thumbs twiddled.

By 8:30, three of the trainees were starting to feel a little rebellious.

"What's up? Where is this jerk? I have plans in the Hamptons and want to get going."

They wanted to leave. Not me. I had already been banished from Goldman once and now I needed the job. Quite simply, I was prepared to stay in the room until Tuesday morning and I said so to my colleagues.

Well, at 9 P.M. the restless three got up and left. They had waited four hours, this guy wasn't coming, and they weren't patsies. They were MBAs from top grad schools, they were future Gordon Gekkos. The rest of us waited.

Finally, at 10 P.M., a Goldman partner, a bit lanky and scrawny, showed up—*five hours late!*

"Hello class," he said, and passed around a sheet of paper on which each of us was to write our name.

When we were done, he said:

So, today's lesson is about waiting patiently for those who are more important than you. Someday you may be in the lobby of a billionaire, and he or she may make you wait. Your job as a representative of Goldman Sachs is to sit there. We are in the client service business. We wait patiently and graciously.

Now, you may have a fancy degree from a fancy place, but that will never replace having the right attitude. Have both and there is nothing that you can't do. Without the right attitude, you are not the right stuff for Goldman Sachs.

Class dismissed.

On Tuesday, the restless three were also dismissed. They were fired from their first jobs. It was a lesson I will never forget. It communicated the culture of the firm without bluster, cheerleading, or empty rhetoric.

Harsh? Absolutely.

Effective? You betcha.

At SkyBridge, we don't use any of those old Goldman techniques. My guess is that era has passed at Goldman, too. The political correctness of our time and the over-lawyering in our culture have probably made training less colorful in all sorts of companies, big and small. Once, I was five minutes late for a training meeting at Goldman. The ensuing conversation went something like this:

"Mr. Scaramucci, do you have a watch?"

"Yes, sir."

"Well the one you have is obviously broken. Go out and get a new watch. We will all wait here for you to get one."

Ever try to find a watch after-hours in the financial district of New York in 1991? Well, guess what? Sweating and running around outside for 20 minutes left me watchless. I had to take the subway to Union Square. My training class compatriots weren't too happy to have me make them wait, squirming in the conference room, for an hour while I searched for my new $5 digital watch. Yet we learned lessons and were forced to pick each other up. It was my turn to be blasted and embarrassed, but we each knew that everyone was going to get their turn. So we stuck together. The training was so good that we forged bonds not only with the firm but with each other.

After training, the absolute best thing that you can do is to put the young people into the fire. Give them the deep end of the responsibility pool. When you can, bring them to meetings so they can witness what you are doing so that they can model this type of behavior in the future. It is also a good idea to make them speak at meetings. Although they may be nervous in the beginning, nothing clarifies thinking more than having to speak in front of your boss, clients, and potential clients.

Among the biggest mistakes that I have made in my career is that I have not provided enough training for my staff or for the people in our underlying companies. The reason? We are a small company, so sometimes it doesn't float up to the highest priority. Lack of time and resources means that we have a focus on things that require an urgent and time-sensitive response. In addition, training typically has no advocate. In the immortal words of Frank Meyer, you need to take on the jobs that have no advocate.

At SkyBridge we are getting better, though. We also try to appeal more to the individual, but I'm thinking hard about the future. Perhaps we can come up with even more innovative and new ways to train people. Maybe one year on Christmas Eve. . . . Nah!

Chapter 7

Teamwork
There's No "I" in Team

Your goal here is to not get fired.
> —*Bob Rubin*

Huh!
> —*Anthony Scaramucci*

When the shamans of Goldman Sachs spoke of the firm's goals and how we could achieve them, they often did so plainly and simply. But when Bob Rubin, who went on to run the firm and ultimately became the Secretary of the Treasury in the Clinton administration, told my training class: "Your goal here is to not get fired," I'll admit to being a bit dumbfounded.

On the thirtieth floor of 85 Broad Street—Goldman Sachs' global corporate headquarters in the storied partner's meeting room—Bob was speaking to a group of young professionals, mostly men, who had achieved and stood out from others their entire lives. They were super-achievers, boy wonders, Eagle Scouts, and favorite sons of their towns. He was asking them merely to survive, to avoid screwing up enough so that they could stick around. But as he explained, it made perfect sense.

You see, Bob believed that the firm was a collection of very talented, self-motivated people. This composition was made possible by a rigorous interview process where prospective employees were often interviewed up to five times to ensure they exhibited a certain skill set and fit the strong Goldman culture. This culture was further supported by training and by retaining a blend that perpetuated an understatement of conceit and an over-statement of collegiality. In other words, once you were part of the family, the collective efforts of its members would penetrate all aspects of your life.

Throughout the orientation, Bob kept referring to the strong culture at Goldman and how we were going to make it even stronger. We were a group that ultimately was quite easy to manage as we were proac-tive, thoughtful, and creative. This combination of intellect, grit, and hard work was to be the engine of growth and prosperity for all of us involved. We were better together. Alone we couldn't get as much accomplished.

His lesson, broadly, was that Goldman was such a great place, ooz-ing talent and brains from every pore, and if you fit in and hung on, you would end up rich and successful. If you left, you were totally on your own in the dog-eat-dog world of Wall Street. It was a posi-tively brilliant and impressionable thing to say: "We are the best and the brightest. Stay here and prosper, leave at your own peril."

But there was another meaning there, too. A way to get fired was to allow your ambition to run amok, to put your own goals before the team's.

When Rubin delivered that line, he wasn't saying to hide in the mail-room so your boss couldn't find and terminate you. He was stressing that each person at the firm had a role. The goal was for each of us to find that role and quietly pursue it to excellence instead of spending time maneuvering against colleagues and griping about our untapped potential.

As normal as that sounds, it is a tough sell. Most of us want some sort of glory. We want to be recognized in some way that defines us as excel-lent or exceptional. Yet up against this is the truth that we need each other.

Throughout this book, I've stressed the importance of following your heart and not losing your soul in pursuit of fortune or fame. It doesn't diminish your accomplishments if you have the maturity and professionalism to be a team player. You can let your passion lead and still communicate with others; you can find your place in the world and be collegial with those you meet along the way—who likely are people you will want or need to be around in the future.

In our businesses, we have to create a dependent, team-oriented culture, straight down from a board of directors who advise us to trusted partners with whom we are mutually invested. To be successful, that network must extend from your family, through your friends, to co-workers and partners. So the big trick in life is figuring out your need for personal glory and balancing it with your ability to get along within your team and be a contributing member.

■ ■ ■

Any person who has or has had a young child has probably heard of the classic *Barney* lyric, "The more we get together, the happier we'll be." Although I'm not a fan of the big purple dinosaur, one of the most central truths in life is that the more we stick together to help each other the better we do.

Sticking together requires ego subordination. One must step out of the spotlight and share. The best companies, the best families, the best sports teams can come together and set aside petty differences. They understand the power of helping each other, pulling for each other rather than competing. Sometimes, however, it requires staying in a shadow, rather than seeking a spotlight.

When I talk to people about this ideal, I frequently point them to Abraham Lincoln's letter to General Hooker, when he commissioned him to run the Army of the Potomac during a critical time—early 1864—in the U.S. Civil War. Lincoln wrote:

> I much fear that the spirit which you have aided to infuse into
> the army, of criticizing their commander and withholding
> confidence from him, will now turn upon you.

Allow me to explain this quote, with a brief history lesson. Hooker had been critical of his superior officer, General Ambrose Burnside, and was working on building his own career by bringing down others. Lincoln knew that Hooker's invective had poisoned the group, but he needed to switch commanders to potentially shake up the initiative in the Army. Having few options, he put his own personal pride aside and appointed General Hooker for the betterment of the group. But he made sure to stress the idea that, less eloquently put, if you crap on people around you, you will start to smell, too. The letter informed Hooker that he now had to command the people he had spent a good amount of time demoralizing. Lincoln's lesson to Hooker: Spare the criticism and focus on the common good. Lincoln's lesson to us: Put aside your differences for the betterment of the group.

War may be a different story, but whether you're part of a sports team or a business, you can almost intuitively feel it when things start to click. People cheer each other on; they are willing to share or do something for each other without a quid pro quo. All of a sudden everybody is driven toward a common goal. The trick to achieving this lies is turning rivalries into cooperation and communication.

Frankly, most teams can't get there. Just a few spoil sports or egotists can spoil the whole team. Michael Jordan, the Hall of Fame Chicago Bulls basketball player, once famously said: "Yeah, there is no 'I' in the word *team*, but there is an 'I' in the word *win*." What does that mean? Simple: individual effort married to the team concept. Jordan, perhaps the greatest basketball player ever, was basically saying that winning took teamwork *and* the individual will. When Jordan got into the league he didn't pass the ball enough and wasn't perceived as a team player, yet over time he subordinated his me-first instincts and the Chicago Bulls started winning. He still remained the guy who wanted the ball in the last seconds of a championship game, but he wanted it because he thought it would benefit the entire team, not just his individual box score.

When I have been asked to lecture students or young trainees on the concept of teamwork, I often refer to Jordan's comment, and I tell them to learn from both of his clichés since both are right. "No 'I' in *team*" means that you need to look around you and figure out what you can do to make the people on your team better every day. Spend time focusing on them and making sure they know that part of your agenda is to see them become successful and that you are going to help them realize their potential. Send a message to each and every one of them that you are pulling for their success.

Jordan's comment that there is an "I" in the word *win* means that you have to work tirelessly on your personal development and personal goals in order to succeed. You have to make sure you are spending time and energy enhancing your skills, practicing, learning new skills, honing your craft, so that when the time comes, you will be the best that you can possibly be. Your contribution to the team can come in many forms, but the main thing is that when it arrives, you have to be prepared to do your best. The individual pursuit of greatness doesn't have to get in the way of contributing to a team.

The uglier side of the Jordan mentality came out in his acceptance speech at the Basketball Hall of Fame years later. He belittled rivals, even those from high school (he even flew one out to the ceremony in Springfield, Massachusetts). It was nasty and laced with bitterness. Words and actions like these signal to people whether you are gearing up for combat or communication and cooperation. Just continue to say to yourself that you can do better. Watch your words, and if you speak for openness and fairness, people will view you as such. If you talk with enthusiasm, people will see your passion.

We need to recognize that the words we say let people know whether we are a team player. How many times have you heard (or even said) the following:

- "I can't believe Jim is making more than me."
- "What? Mary is just terrible at her job. How is she getting that promotion?"

- "Let's face it: I am smarter and more talented than you, and I can't understand how you are doing better."
- "I sold 20 units this month. No one cares about you and what you do."
- "That jerk has an office and I have a cubicle?!"

This is corrosive language for a team. Immediately, the social signal sent out by this person's words is picked up on everyone's transmitter: This is the sort of someone who can't embrace and enjoy the success of others. This person only cares about himself, never thinks about making a sacrifice or lending a helping hand to another. This transparently competitive behavior and language is antisocial and impels others to cast the "You're off the island" vote.

So it is important that you carefully watch your words and use inclusive and positive language. One way to do so is to put yourself in the position of the owner of a business or the leader of a team. In this role, ask yourself, "How would the person next to me benefit in what I am doing right now? How can I teach or potentially help the people around me? Am I fair and cordial to people or do I bark orders when I think I have power over somebody?"

Make yourself proud; display the best side of yourself even when you are squaring off with your most bitter rivals. Yes, every team has a few bad apples and it is going to be impossible to like every person on a team, but don't let that ruin your behavior. Be the role model for others and, lo and behold, you will become one.

And here's another news flash: If you are a "Me" sort of person, it isn't the end of the world—you just have to work on it. It requires self-awareness, training, and a redirection of habits. Here are three quick ideas:

1. Spend time with your teammates, learning how best to help them.
2. A few unselfish acts go a long way. No one is expecting you to be a saint, but if you come up with a few acts of graciousness and kindness people will notice it.

3. Don't spend time in the nasty gossip zone. I don't know why, but people love to gripe and find reasons to put each other down. Sometimes we feel we have to be in the group of carpers so that people around us accept us into their clique. Don't let this be you. It is destructive and poisonous to be part of the negative cabal. Avoid it—even if that makes you seem snooty or uppity to certain people. Who cares?

It is important that you are deemed to be part of the positive crowd and a positive influence on others. You don't have to fit into the crowd if the crowd is a bunch of losers. Over time you will quietly earn the respect of those around you. The ones whose respect you haven't earned will eventually find their way to the door. Either good management will weed them out or they will wilt and end up leaving. Time and time again, I have watched negative people job-hop, always thinking that they will find the perfect place, but of course they never do because they don't spend enough time making their teams better. Winning and whining may look like cousins on a page, but they never go together.

■ ■ ■

There will always be internal squabbles on a team; the seeds of dissension always get sown a bit. Some people feel they do more than others; another group may feel underappreciated. Throughout my career, I have been in situations where the lazy partner takes advantage of the action-oriented partner. The boss, who believes he's risen above the crowd by rolling up his sleeves, dumps work incessantly on energized underlings. Every company has a share of workers and a share of slackers. There are things that can be done to put an end to this sort of nonsense, but it requires an ability to accept some conflict and, if necessary, confront some people.

Goldman Sachs was a place that understood this and still does. In an industry loaded with stars and big egos, the most talented people are attracted to Goldman and its ways. Despite the current negative populist sentiment against Goldman many young people want to work there. Don't believe me? Just ask any business major or MBA student where they want to work when they graduate. When I graduated, I was lucky to work there.

When I arrived at Goldman in 1989, John L. Weinberg was the senior partner in the firm. His father, Sidney Weinberg, was famous for starting in the firm's mailroom and helping the firm survive the economic depression of the 1930s. John had inherited his father's gift to be a trusted adviser to CEOs from around the world. Also, he was a man who practiced what he preached and loved to "eat the cooking of his clients." For instance, since the firm took the Ford Motor Company public in 1956, he drove a Ford. Because Goldman Sachs took Sears public in 1906, John shopped at Sears.

At the core of all of his actions was his belief that teamwork enabled the firm to reach their objectives. He said, "The point is this team thing, the cooperation, the teamwork, and our culture was developed not because someone was a genius and woke up in the middle of the night when the little electric light popped. It really came from the needs of the moment. It's good, solid business. You want to have people working together to achieve an objective."

It was a message that was lived from the very top of the firm back in those days. He and John Whitehead started the tradition of Goldman being led by two people. Imagine, in the world's most ego-driven, me-first business, having two very talented senior people subordinate their egos for the betterment of the group! That was quintessential Goldman, and within it a quintessential lesson.

It was a powerful feeling to be part of something so purposeful. A person could quickly find themselves excised if they were acting against the firm or the interests of others. There was no fooling around on these issues, and the firm's best people were capable of calling a person out on the negativity, lack of sportsmanship, or lack of team play. Weed out the bottom 10 percent and ensure the other 90 percent focus and, as a bonus, reduce resentment about someone else getting a free ride.

The Goldman guys got it. Mark O. Winkelman, who was once the head of fixed income there, used to remind us that our rivals on the Street had the same desks, the same phones, and the same computers. The only way to get ahead of them was to stick together.

When John Whitehead left the firm to become an Undersecretary of State in the Reagan administration, Weinberg was atop the firm by himself. He was the real deal—earthy, not pretentious, unassuming, but incredibly tough. He wanted the firm to move as one. Even the most cliché Gordo Gekko bankers—the ones with the slicked-back hair, suspenders, custom suits, custom shirts, custom shoes, and custom egos to match—had a hard time acting like an ass in front of him. His stare was capable of calling you out on it. His lack of status conscious-ness showed he was the most powerful and the most respected. It was from him that we all learned how to use pronouns, and he urged us to drop "I" and "me" from our vernacular.

And if Weinberg's partners were quarreling, Weinberg would bel-low: "Leave history to the historians, let's get back to work." He hated blame exercises and finger pointing; he didn't care who was right, he wanted the argument to stop. He had the gravitas, too, to get the argu-ment to end. This is the best truism of success: Don't let something petty overpower the ultimate common goal.

His message: Focus on *we*, *our*, *together*, and *us*. Pronouns send powerful messages. What are yours? Watch them carefully. Sure, all of us have been guilty of the "me/I" thing. We aren't really aware of the corrosive effect it can have on our relationships because it is so subtle. Yet say it often enough, and people will be less inclined to want to be with you. Be careful. You must practice this. Want to get ahead? Don't focus on being a star; do your work without any grandiosity, and you will find the highest perch. Be self-effacing and low-key; cooperate, and better the people around you. Want the spotlight? You can go work somewhere else—at some Wall Street shop or company where they will eat each other alive. One face to the client, seamless and interchangeable—that should be the goal of the firm where you want to work.

So here is the mantra: I will take a piece of myself and give it to the team as I know our sum is greater than each of us individually. Also, if possible, I will try to resist the urge to compete with my lateral teammates.

It's unwise to have Gordon Gekko's view of business and think of it as a zero-sum game. You just have to have faith that there is plenty of money, achievement, and status to be had out there for everybody. Trust in that and try to help your peers rather than hurt them. It's so simple to say, so hard to do. It's hard to do because it goes against many of our primordial survival instincts and it is counter to our need to stand out. As Gekko says, "Greed captures the essence of the evolutionary spirit." Yet being able to successfully play on a team is one of the ultimate secrets to great success. It is one of the secrets to happiness too, as it gives all of us a higher sense of purpose.

■■■

The concept of teamwork can be applied everywhere and on every level. It can improve the dynamic in a family as well as the dynamic of the world. Or maybe the way a person contributes to a family can improve the dynamic of a business and the world as it teaches him how to be a contributing, yet connective, member. That was certainly true in my case.

When I was five years old, my grandmother—my mom's mom, known to me as Nana—used to help me get ready for kindergarten. She was an Italian immigrant and had a tough time with English even though at that point she'd been in the United States for 46 years.

Her morning ritual: Get me dressed, make me eggnog (raw eggs—no salmonella threat back then), and get me on the school bus. One morning I was late and I ran from the house without kissing her goodbye. This was unacceptable. She followed me out of the house, stepped in front of the bus, came aboard and—to my great embarrassment in front of my pals—made me kiss her goodbye. It was an expression of love and determination that I will never forget.

My Nana was always concerned about the continuity of family and wanted us to stick together, so she instilled certain values in us. They were simple things: Watch out for each other, and make sure that you do your best to treat everybody with respect. She was certain that "what goes around comes around" and made it clear to us that if we did bad things, then bad things would happen to us. There was a karmic justice in her universe and she wanted us to abide by it. She also, however, didn't want us to take any bullshit.

When I was seven, a neighborhood bully decided to pick on me. He wanted me to leave the ball field so he teased me and called me names. When he began chasing me with a rope that he was swinging like a whip over his head, I ran right into my house, cowering. Nana looked at me and asked what was going on. When I told her, she told me to go outside, make a fist and without saying a word, punch the bully right in the nose. What? I was scared shitless. This kid was two years older than me and a lot stronger, bigger too. I said no way.

You see, I was hoping that she was going to go out there and protect me, possibly even tattle on him to his mom. But she didn't do this. Instead, she adamantly said I had to go outside and get the job done. "Better to learn now to stick up for yourself," she said.

With tears in my eyes and sweaty palms, I marched over to the baseball field. I walked up to the bully, stared at him and popped him as hard as I possibly could. Then I jumped on him and began punching away. He was caught off guard, started to cry, and ran into his house.

The next day when we saw each other, he acted like it had never happened, but he was dramatically friendlier. A bully cowed.

Oddly enough, this was an invaluable lesson for me. Now I can spot bullies a mile away—they are the people usually dealing with all sorts of insecurities and shortcomings, and almost always can be brought down through the deterrence of strength. More importantly, on that day I learned how to hold my ground and stick up for myself, all the while garnering the respect of my grandmother. These are the seeds a young person needs to grow into the leader of a team—a leader who listens to the advice of experienced others and courageously fights for what is right. All of this guided me from playing on the sports team right up to being the managing partner at SkyBridge.

■■■

Not only did my Nana teach me how to deal with bullies—I mean, be a leader—she also taught me about the importance of family and sticking together. We didn't like everything about each other, but we were a family.

Every Sunday, my Nana would cook Sunday dinner—tons of macaroni, meatballs, and gravy. And every Sunday, her 13 grandchildren would sit together in her little living room and eat until we were ready to explode. Although we didn't know it then, it was at that folding table where we all bonded. To this day, most of us are very close and try to look out for each other.

There is power in such community and togetherness. Our community needs to come together more and collectively address our problems. Our work and lifestyles have drawn us apart but we have lots of things in common, and we need to step forward again and identify what they are so that we can become stronger as a unit. Other generations made the sacrifices; it's our turn now.

Now, I know my grandmother is no Lincoln, Churchill, or Weinberg. However, great leaders come in many different forms, but they all have one thing in common: They believe in the power of teamwork to achieve a successful outcome. Lincoln's goal was preserving the United States of America, so he made it clear to Hooker that the team needed him to achieve something beyond his own ambitions. Weinberg's goal was unifying a bunch of analysts at Goldman Sachs by having them subordinate their ego. And my grandmother's goal—as with many Italian-Americans—was preserving the family unit that for thousands of years back home had been threatened by foreign invasions.

We are all on teams—as citizens in our country, as employees in a business, as members in a family. How we perform within them can determine their ability to survive.

You have to make the commitment to others. The survival of a country and its ideals, the advancement of an idea and culture, the continuity of a family—it all requires the same shared commitment. It is a force that can really shape our world and change our future. At some point we must start to recognize that we are all in this together.

■ ■ ■

A central idea of teamwork is putting aside your differences for the betterment of the group. Although this is primarily a book on how to become successful in business without sacrificing yourself to the god of greed, it is important to recognize that you also have a role in the society that you live in. You need to do things for your community, country, and world that make life better for the people around you.

Since *teamwork* can be defined as "spirited, common collaboration," it can apply to all sorts of social systems. Teamwork can be used to reach objectives in the boardroom, the schoolyard, the White House, and maybe even someday in the UN. But it's hard for us. People have a tendency to put their own needs first. When others see this sort of self-gratifying behavior, they immediately stoop to that level and gravitate toward their combative and competitive nature.

In arguably one of his best speeches, President John F. Kennedy said on June 10, 1963, that we could achieve world peace if the citizens of the world pulled together. Here are some of his words:

I am talking about genuine peace, the kind of peace that makes life on earth worth living, the kind that enables men and nations to grow and to hope and to build a better life for their children; not merely peace for Americans but peace for all men and women; not merely peace in our time but peace for all time. . . .

So let us not be blind to our differences—but let us also direct attention to our common interests and to the means by which those differences can be resolved. And if we cannot end now our differences, at least we can help make the world safe for diversity. For, in the final analysis, our most basic common link is that we all inhabit this small planet. We all breathe the same air. We all cherish our children's future. And we are all mortal.

In this speech at American University, JFK eloquently captured people's commonalities and appealed to each of us as citizens of the world, not just of our own country. His basic message: We are all in this together; we all share common bonds—*all* of us. So let's work together to make life better for one and for all. Simply put, he promoted teamwork.

Yet the current generation of American politicians practice polarization and obfuscation. Here are a few things you won't be hearing from this irresponsible crew:

- "We need to cut your Social Security benefits—we can't afford all of the benefits that you have been promised."
- "We have over $60 trillion in forward liabilities if you want to throw in pension fund, health care, and other sorts of entitlements. This amount will bankrupt the United States."
- "Once we start a government project it takes on a life of its own and never dies, no matter the cost or the effectiveness."

There are so many other truths that won't be heard. As a result, most of the American population is starting to express anxiety and unrest as it relates to the programs or initiatives that will negatively affect their own lives. In a sense, they feel betrayed—after all, they elected public officials to work for them, but now it somehow feels like they are only working to promote their own political agendas.

This is a recipe for disaster. This is the essence of a team dismantling.

Although political leaders should enforce higher and nobler actions, they often reinforce this type of independent, me-first behavior through their actions or lack thereof. In the United States, partisan divisions seem to run deep, or at least that is how it is portrayed by the media. For instance, potential solutions to the economic crisis ran into road-blocks on each political side. As President Obama struggled through these and other early tests in the White House, voices on the right cried "socialism" at every turn, while voices on the left remained disappointed when insurance companies and medical giants were pulled into the debate over the nation's looming health care crisis.

The better part of us knows that there are certain things that we can do to promote social justice and equal opportunities. Such ideals aren't from the Democrats or the Republicans; they are universally American. That leaves most of us sitting in the middle with more practical centrist leanings, where we stand for equal rights, equal opportunity, social choice but also free markets and capitalism. We don't overspend in our checkbooks and on credit cards, and we find it reckless when the government uncontrollably overspends on programs and initiatives.

Yet, for some reason, all we hear are the voices of the extremists.

Debate is fine. It is the most American part of America—but hate speech, couched racism and homophobia, and shock-doctrine tactics aren't. The freedom that the United States built faster and better than any other society in history lies in the balance. Perhaps it requires some subordination for each of us to make it all work better, just like on any team. Perhaps we need more effective leadership—one that is better in its representation of our core values, rather than dedicated to the proposition of political expediency.

Remember, we are better off together. If we look to the sum of our efforts—not only the tax rates on the rich or the struggles of our relatively comfortable middle class—we can accomplish great things.

■ ■ ■

You've all heard the story and read the history books: In 1776, a group of aristocratic white men, mostly deists, got together to declare that "all men are created equal" and are endowed to certain unalienable rights, including the right to life, liberty, and the pursuit of happiness. They drafted these ideals into the Declaration of Independence and the Constitution, which has since been used to govern our republican democracy. While there are times when it feels like we are getting close to realizing these ideals, there are other times when it feels like we are getting further and further away from them.

Freedom, as our forefathers envisioned it, is like art. As an artist expresses her creativity, painting life on a fresh alabaster canvas, she is free to take it wherever she wants. America was conceived to represent these ideals: We have open dissent, we have candid expression, and we can shape our lives and destinies as we please. We move freely interstate and we use the same currency, which makes us the most powerful free-trading bloc in the world.

This is not the case in other countries. In the global society, people's right to exercise their own free will has been at odds with the rules and doctrines of certain governments. Thus, the United States has become known as the land of opportunity, a place where a person can achieve freedom, equality, and progress for the next generation. Our nation invited everybody (well, almost everybody) to share in this American Dream. In the process, we spilled each other's blood on battlefields, southern streets, and college campuses, and fought even bloodier wars on foreign soil. We broke the back of Nazism and imperial Japan, then rebuilt big portions of two continents. Not long after, we took on Communism in its worst iteration and prevailed in a way that made the entire world safer for more than a decade. Along the way, we have offered political refuge to the persecuted, protection to the embattled, and personal freedom to the forsaken. Yet America is currently better known for giving the world Wall Street scandals, Brangelina, and childhood obesity. How unfortunate.

Think about the precedents and accomplishments America sets. The last president did more for Africa than any other in history. In 2009, we elected an African-American president. Embarrassingly, I didn't realize the significance of such an achievement until I was told so by a Kuwaiti client and friend. In the midst of business negotiations in London, we began talking about President Obama and his initiatives. He said, "Anthony, you have no idea what this means to the world. In many countries he couldn't become a citizen, much less a President, because his father was not a native."

President Obama has often said that his story could not have happened in any place other than America. Yet it took a foreigner in a foreign country to tell me—a proud American—that my country is constantly renewing, reinventing, and realizing dreams. Our actions over time will match our ideals, and when they do the society will be richer and better. It takes all of us pulling together to make that happen, just like on any team.

The world is listening. Are you?

■ ■ ■

Despite the most lofty of ideals and most eloquent pronouncements from that original group of white guys and our secular messiah Lincoln, we have not lived up to our ideals of treating all men equal. In fact, we fought a civil war, experienced a decade of protests in the streets, inserted several amendments to the Constitution, made several Supreme Court rulings, and marched on Washington, all in an effort to allow men to be treated equal. In some parts of the country in the 1960s we turned fire hoses on blacks marching for their total freedom and an end to segregation. The hatred and fear were pervasive. Skin color meant perceived inferiority or superiority. It was all about the color of skin without regard to the content of character.

Why was this so? It's Darwinian; it's tribal. Tribal societies believed in survival of the fittest. In order to survive, they believed that they had to surround themselves with people who had the most in common with them—whether it be the same eye, skin, or hair color; language and idioms; or cultural customs. When these tribes became nations, they typically warred with those who looked different from them.

And for a long time, the whites ruled supreme. They took over black lands and enslaved their people. Consequently, they created a nation separated by skin color and physical attributes.

There is one human race; there isn't a black race or a white race. We see the walls of color coming down across our society, in the arts, in the statehouses, and with a new generation to whom color doesn't seem to be defining. Yet we still have racism; we just don't have the courage to admit it. That's a problem. We need to courageously expose racism on both sides of the color spectrum and open it up more forcefully to debate and dialogue.

Thankfully, there have been those courageous ones among us who have sought to level the playing field. Dr. Martin Luther King Jr. attempted to end racial segregation and discrimination through civil disobedience. Jackie Robinson, the consummate team player, was spat on, barked at, and ridiculed, but he broke the color barrier. These are just two examples of generational teamwork—sacrificing oneself for the betterment of the team's future. Think about it, without Dr. King and Jackie, there is likely no Oprah, no Obama, no Arthur Ashe.

The reality is that none of us picked anything about ourselves—not our IQs, our height, our skin color, or the places we were born. Yet so often we judge one another on these random biological assignments. We are all accidents of nature, yet as long as such things shape our destinies, total freedom feels elusive.

It is time to move on from racial divides. We need to stop these shallow judgments. We need to pull together as one team and work together. Heck, many American citizens teamed up together and elected the first black president of the United States. We are not there yet, but if we are united in our effort to reach this destination, we will be. We are in it together. We are one team.

Think post-tribal. America is a land that is consistently moving toward a post-tribal way of life. It is setting an example for the future. Hopefully someday we will be looked at as creating the precursor for the post-tribal world. One tribe, the human tribe. One race, the human race. That would be the apotheosis of teamwork. We can do this. We have to force ourselves to be brave enough. Have the courage to stop fearing each other, the strength to recognize our similarities, our commonalities, not our differences. None of us are true strangers. We have lots in common.

This sounds utopian and perhaps wildly idealistic, but think about the past 500 years and think about the progress we have made in our society. Think about how much better the world is when we are collaborating. The need for the protection of tribes is ending as we expand our ability to understand the world that we inhabit.

■■■

The United States remains a nation in progress, just like a masterpiece that takes years to create. It meanders toward an ideal, needs some lines to be shaded and others to be erased, but mostly it needs its creation to flow freely and be expressed in ways we often haven't yet considered.

Sometimes you have to be from a different county—such as my friend from Kuwait—to appreciate what America is, and sometimes you have to be reminded of our core values in simple, everyday situations.

It's a lot like my grandmother's lessons. She probably knew that my life would be better than hers, but she knew I needed the support of my family—my team—to get there. Members of a family—like citizens of a nation, like employees of a company—need to recognize the others who belong to it and work with them to reach their collective goals.

As we push toward a post-tribal society, it is important to understand the concepts of teamwork and fair play. It is impossible to win everyone over, but we must remain optimistic and practice what we preach, just like the legendary John Weinberg.

America's greatest moments, like those of our family or workplace, are laced with simplicity, teamwork, and cooperation. This country of ours has always been willing to make sacrifices for its ideals. We are woven together more by these concepts than the location of our origin. While America is not entirely post-tribal and is quite far from perfect, let's look toward its progress with some level of pride and satisfaction and strive to make improvements for its future. Let's work together to promote equality and demonstrate, through our words and actions, that all men are created equal and should be treated as such. We have not been pulling together like we used to. It's time to start being a team again.

Chapter 8

The People You Meet on the Street

You Take the Good, You Take the Bad

I hate nobody but Hitler, and that's professional.
—*Winston Churchill*

S o there was the time—earlier in my career, between the cheap suit phase and the golden era—during which I worked with an insidious business partner. He was someone who was always overnegotiating, overreaching on a deal, acting like a completely selfish pig. He always needed to be associated with important people, and routinely Windexed the lesser ones, both of which made him simply a horrific person to be around. I'll refrain from using his name, but he was famous for a callous insensitivity to others about which his *faux* friends (yep, including me) would nervously laugh, and to this day I am still embarrassed by it. He spent much of his time hiding behind the glamour of his art collection and the prestige of his position. Yet, against my better judgment, I teamed up with this person because he was working with a prestigious group. I thought there was a way for me to control the situation—that I could be the person's friend and, through the friendship, steer the business relationship to common ground and fairness.

I was wrong.

At some point I came to a harsh realization: The guy had no friends. He had hangers-on who thought, because of his status and some of the fun things he does, they should hang out with him. I was there doing the same things, talking myself into all of it. I didn't fully want to understand the situation and I let my self-talk override my instincts. This is why I am so certain that money corrupts and that situations can cloud your judgment.

In hindsight, I realize I actually could feel the evil, but I rationalized that the evil was necessary and the rewards would be big. One of my mentors, Bob Castrignano, told me I should stay away from the guy. I didn't listen—at least not at first. After I eventually extricated myself from the situation, a friend of mine (someone I truly respected) left me stung when he said he was "happy" for me for getting out of the deal, and that he had begun to doubt *my* character for being hooked up with the other guy.

The truth hurt. Perhaps it was personal insecurity that caused me to team up with the bad guy, who really knows? What I learned, however, was that I was unable to compromise too much of my character and lose my soul in pursuit of wealth. People still work with this other guy. They still make money and have nice homes and huge apartments. And they are still miserable.

Churchill, at least, was clever. Spend enough time on Wall Street and you run into all stripes of people. Most irksome among them is the shark who, paraphrasing a line from *The Godfather*, will slaughter those around him for sport and claim, "It's just business. It's not personal." I call this group "The Great Chiselers." Like Gordon Gekko, they only understand the game as win-lose; they think social occasions are only meant to be opportunities to measure themselves against others based only on their bank accounts, cars, and second wives.

These are the sort of people that Oliver Stone was thinking about when he said to a *New York Times* reporter during the shooting of *Wall Street: Money Never Sleeps* that he "didn't like glorifying pigs." In fact, these were the people who could've benefited from Li Ka-shing's lesson to leave money on the table for my partners. The one hitch in those sage words: If you meet this sort of chiseler he won't only take the money you leave; he will reach in your pocket and try to find a way to get more.

My philosophy is simple: Do business with people you like and trust. Some people on Wall Street think that's weak. Those Gekko wannabes are the same people who would advise always playing hardball, but then proceed to tear out your eyeballs and suck your skull, laughing the whole time.

They may justify their actions and say, "It's not personal, it's just business." In fact, to them, your gestures of fairness or kindness are almost like a green light to rip your heart out. The fact that you might allow it sort of gets them off, makes them feel superior. And yeah, the likelihood is that they will be richer than you, but only if you measure fortune in dollars and cents.

More often than not these people have dysfunctional personal relationships and are lonely or unhappy. And therein lies the dirty little secret about business: You can't really separate it from your true personality. If you spend 80 hours each week acting like a ruthless moron, you can't just turn it off when you go home. There's no chance of that happening. Your darkness comes through the door with you and so does your diabolical callousness. You may get rich, but you will be filled with acid and acrimony. How could that be worth it? Screw enough people and the karma police come and take out all of your flesh. These people build up resentments around them and then invariably something bad happens—a chink in their armor, an exposure, and before you know it they get toasted.

I will never, ever buy the "It's just business" argument. We spend too much of our life in business and working with others to grow our companies, produce profits, and help the people and families associated with us succeed. When you say "It's just business," it's code for "I am going to try to take your eyes out."

It's complicated, sometimes, to explain to people what is wrong with this pattern of behavior. Herman Melville, the famous American novelist who wrote *Moby Dick*, once wrote:

> We cannot live only for ourselves. A thousand fibers connect us with our fellow men [and women]; and among those fibers, as sympathetic threads, our actions run as causes, and they come back to us as effects.

You'd think that our centuries as humans would allow us to figure that out—that a person's positive connection to others is what contributes to his overall happiness and ultimately defines him. The trouble for some people on Wall Street, however, is that the greed and the accompanying status are so intoxicating that it can cause a person to sign a Faustian pact. Why not? It requires a couple of sacrifices but the riches are guaranteed—they were even after Wall Street collapsed in 2008. As the U.S. TARP bill (Troubled Assets Relief Program) was put into the equation, and the government socialized losses and ultimately allowed the banks to start paying large bonuses again. But once again I digress. The essentials of this pact are evident: Aggregate together. Live near each other, spend summer in the same areas, send your kids to the same schools, and spend each day and night positioning yourself for more and for higher status.

Years ago, when I was working at Goldman, there was a guy who got up at 5 A.M. to run around the Central Park reservoir with a senior partner. He even bought the partner a running vest, as if any Goldman partner needed anyone buying anything for them, short of a private island. It was classic, like the little kid bringing the teacher a shiny red apple, a total abandonment of pride and self-determination. Apply lips to cheek, suck, and kiss (see, I told you it is a sucker's game). And we know why it happens: money.

Here's the thinking: "You mean I can be rich for the rest of my life and all I have to do is sit in this seat, answer these certain phone calls, make sure I don't ever offend upper management, and I can have it all?" For most this is an easy question to answer. Play the game, be in the inside crowd, and make a ton of dough. The problem with this is that it ultimately creates a vicious circle. The personality morphs. There is always a series of compromises and behavior modifications. Speak up? Nope. Be real? Can't do that, either. The gear—clothing, accessories like a wife, kids, and a big house—all have to be inside the circle of conformity.

■ ■ ■

So bankers come in a standard size. Although there are many socially responsible people on Wall Street, the perception that they are morally corrupt, arrogant bastards has become a reality in many ways. In general no one cared that they were getting rich. It was part of the American Dream to do so.

When they blew up the financial system and had to get bailed out with taxpayers' money, however, it was time to break out the pitchforks and torches. They can take down the financial system, then appear incredulous that other people are angry with them. They demand high bonuses after the debacle with the zeal and smugness of the entitled, and then expect the media and the rest of the country to return to the status quo of lionizing their lives and lifestyle.

There is a name for what they did. It's called malpractice. Imagine a community of doctors causing disease or a pestilence. Where would all of the trial lawyers be? These guys acted in a reckless manner that almost destroyed the global financial system, and if you think about it from the malpractice framework, then why don't they have insurance to cover their self-created disasters?

The anger, frankly, is understandable.

I do think Wall Street will make a comeback in the eyes of Main Street but it will take a while. Most people are disgusted and angry, maybe more than at any time in recent memory. They have seen the Gekko wannabes blow up the financial system, trigger fear and panic, and knock 10 percent of America out of jobs. They have pushed their illusions so far, to such as garish level, that it is now obvious to most people they have traded their decency for the almighty dollar.

Yet I am certain that there are good people who are working at big Wall Street banks. I know many of them. What I am far less certain of is the presence of any shred of self-awareness in these other Masters of the Universe. Could they really be this tone-deaf? Could they love money so much and be so intoxicated and self-absorbed that the calamity that they contributed to could hold no guilt for them? It's odd.

The people on the Street need to react to the anger in a way that people can relate to. A real apology and real positive social action would go a long way on Main Street—not a staged, half-baked one presented by their damage-control PR firm. Until they do that there will be continued political and social fury.

Now, I am all for success and I would never suggest that we regulate away high earners; bonuses are terrific as they encourage hard work and merit incentives. I am also not sitting around feeling that we should tie down our economy through overregulation, pay czars, and other sorts of things that appease the angry masses in the short run. However, what I am saying is that the role of social purpose and social conscience are now creeping into the society. That's a good thing. We are at a true inflection point. Having a house that can be profiled in *Architectural Digest*, dying rich and lonely, surrounded by your art and material trappings may no longer be a virtue—it's a cancer.

Our standard issue is that the mentality of many successful people on Wall Street is contributing to the new plague of inequality. Do they get it? We shall see.

■ ■ ■

So where does all this greed come from? How do people become like this? And what can you do to avoid these pitfalls in your own life?

For starters, if you work for one of these banks and you think that there is any credence to what I am saying, ask yourself: Will a group inside your firm rebel and go to senior management and file a formal complaint? I think not. Moreover, it is probably the opposite: It would be politically unacceptable and career damaging to challenge the status quo. What is the price you place on your own personal conformity? The passion that you feel for life and the challenge of trying to do the right thing—is that for sale?

My point is that this behavior starts somewhere in an organization and it is perpetuated through passivity and the fear of speaking up. And it's no different than life outside the office.

Here's another internal test for you: Who is your best friend? Is it a neighbor? A co-worker? A classmate? Think for a moment what makes that person your best, most favored, most trusted compatriot. For me, the definition of the best comes not only from love and trust, but from an ingredient so rare it needs to be cherished and nurtured. What is it?

Celebration.

There are too many people on Wall Street who are just wired to not like it when someone else is doing well. It drives them crazy. The full moon for the Wall Street werewolf is the sight of a peer making a killing in business. Nasty stuff. They can't stand seeing others succeed and often will transparently expose their envy, greed, and narcissism. But here are a couple of ways to think about the type of person you need to be, to be more happy and successful in your life.

Always be known as a person who can cheer about the success of others. There is a funny thing about life—you can hear the right words coming out of a person's mouth, but see from their body language or feel from their intonations that they just don't mean it. It's shallow, gratuitous support.

Don't ever be the party pooper who always has something negative to say, or that phony colleague who transparently pretends they are happy for someone else's success. Be bigger. Know that there is true joy in expressing happiness for someone else's career success. Realize that if you can tell when someone is faking it, chances are they can tell when you are, too.

When a person can celebrate with you and genuinely be enthusiastic about your success and achievements without any hidden envy or jealousy, it is the most powerful adhesive for a friendship. As kids we all heard the expression, "If you want a friend, *be* a friend," and it makes sense that the most special of our friends are those who can jump for joy alongside of us. Think of the person you want to call first when you have good news. Think of how special that person makes you feel. Are you that person in anyone's life? I have that person in mine.

I know a man who probably has 900 people in his life who call him their best friend. He is so kindhearted and warm that if the angel Lucifer walked into the bar he would say, "Hey, Lou, can I get you something?" There's not a trace of malice in him, just all kindness and respect. There is a terrific dignity about those among us who can celebrate the success of others and be thought of as a person who would drop everything to lend a helping hand.

Living like that takes a certain type of courage. And to do the right thing by some, you often have to challenge others.

It's not always easy. In fact, often it's quite difficult. It would be elitist and arrogant to suggest you can simply walk away from bosses and situations that can compromise your character. The greater danger is trying to rationalize it. Take Gordon Gekko. Although I have pointed out his despicable behaviors throughout this book, to many people who saw the film in the 1980s the character was a likeable rogue and grew into a cultural icon. Even Oliver Stone has been surprised by the public's sentiment toward the character. Gekko was morally deplorable, yet there were entire classes of MBA students in the 1980s and 1990s who would tell you that the moral ambiguity of his life was a fair trade for his lavish lifestyle. To me that's unbelievable, but let's take a few minutes and more carefully examine the ways of the wayward Wall Street warrior.

The Gekko-like, Wall Street bad guy is absorbed only with his own success, and could really care less about anything or anybody else.

Guys like this believe in Gekko's mantra, "If you need a friend, get a dog." Yet it is really bad for us when they are in our friendship circle or workplace. Instead of taking steroids, their performance is enhanced by their narcissism and their ability to act in a way that normal, honorable people do not. They actually understand this and they use it against the people who are trying to play fairly. That's patently disgusting, right? Well, at one time or another we, due to our better natures, have tried to cut this sort of person some slack. It happens because we are trying to convince ourselves and others that one of those types "isn't *that* bad" or because we need something from them, or maybe we work for them. It's like the Stockholm syndrome, where hostages fall in love with their captors.

For instance, toward the climax of the original *Wall Street* film, it is apparent that the evolving Bud Fox knows of Gekko's illegal and unethical behaviors, yet he tries to justify them because he wants to achieve Gekko's approval and be rich enough to have his own jet and be "a player." Bud even stoops so low as to tell his own loving, blue-collar father, who is trying to help Bud see that Gekko is using him, that he's is just a "jealous old machinist who can't stand that his son has become more successful than he has!"

Like Bud, there have been many times in life when I have found myself rationalizing an existing relationship, as in the case I described at the beginning of the chapter. I was fortunate never to really work for this sort of boss. My first partner, Andrew K. Boszhardt Jr., was a gem, and so is my current partner, Scott Prince, but I have had my share of bad guys who have either been my clients or have owned pieces of my businesses over the years. The gut tells you, "No! Run! Get away from this person!" Yet too often I have rationalized the situation and stayed.

It might not be that bad of a deal if you could just shake that kind of behavior off. But you can't. A situation like that just kills something inside you and creates wear and tear on your soul. There's no justification or excuse for the experience. After you cut loose, hindsight makes the need obvious. Ask a smoker after they have kicked the habit if smoking is that good of an idea when examined against the damage it could do. The mind will actually clear faster than the lungs. Cutting bad people out of your life isn't very different. Not only is it liberating, it's better for your karma and health.

I realize it's not easy. We are human and we worry about our paychecks and our job security. But too much compromise can be a dangerous thing. We spend many of our waking hours at work. It's important that we be surrounded and supervised by people who recognize that each and every one of us is something special.

If you are leading an organization, don't let one employee within your domain ever feel that you are insensitive to the challenges that they face in their life. Even if you let a person go, you can do it with care and concern. To Gordon Gekko, people like Buddy were like disposable toilet paper—a cockroach, a nobody. If they were doing something for him, great; if not, it was on to the next vulnerable up-and-comer.

It is not about being liked by everyone. In fact, sometimes I take great pleasure in having certain people be detractors of me or of our business; your enemies can define you, too, as with Churchill and Hitler. It's okay if bad guys say bad things about you, but what about the rest of us? Be the type of person who will have people there to lift you in tough times.

But, for all you Gordon Gekko wannabes, we're on to you, and here are some of the illnesses that you may suffer:

- **The Harder They Fall Syndrome.** This is a shout-out to those who step on people's fingers on the way to the top of the corporate ladder. Be careful not to fall, because there could be a line of people waiting to pile on. Former New York Governor Eliot Spitzer discovered that his harsh, intimidating tactics came home to roost when his own judgment faltered. After he became a hooker's Client No. 9, I don't recall anyone jumping on the airwaves to give sympathetic testimonials for Spitzer. In fact, the self-made billionaire Ken Langone, whom Spitzer had sued and publicly lambasted while Attorney General, went on CNBC and said: "We all have somewhere inside us our own personal hell. I hope Eliot's is worse than others." Contrast that with George Bailey, the character so famously portrayed by Jimmy Stewart in the 1946 movie *It's a Wonderful Life*. When he was in trouble, the neighbors to whom he'd been loyal and kind rallied to his side. The best thing to do is start out and finish up by being nice.

- **The Ninth Circle of Hell: Living with the Devil.** In Dante's classic, *The Inferno*, he defines hell for us mortals. There are nine levels and depending on your crime to humanity you earn a different spot or station. The ninth circle, the lowest depths of hell, is cold, a frozen lake around which lurks the Devil and those who have committed the worst crime known to humankind. For Dante this circle is full of people who have betrayed their friends, so among the celebrities residing in the Ninth Circle are Judas, the betrayer of Christ (God and Faith); and Brutus and Cassius, the assassins of Julius Caesar (metaphorically the State, but also friendship). I'm thinking the Devil is going to be working the late shift sometime 30 to 40 years from now when most of these Wall Street cads die. And sometime sooner, he will be greeting the master of all betrayers: Bernard Madoff. Madoff is one of history's greatest rogues. He took money from friends, charities, holocaust survivors, and anyone and any organization that would feed his scheme. This despicable behavior and social pathology is actually born from self-hatred.

  My biggest mistake thus far (and I am confident there will be many more) was thinking someone was a friend and having him betray me. It was a great learning experience. To gain some measure of self-satisfaction, I registered the URL, www.9thcirclecapitalmanagement.com, for this guy; this way when he eventually falls out of his prestigious job he will have a new business to go to.

- **The "I Should Have Been a Contender" Syndrome.** This is a classic. The storyline sort of goes like this: I am really smart, went to the best schools, have a great pedigree, so how is it possible I am not doing better? I should be one of the kings, a titan on Wall Street. The truth is a lot of people have all the right ingredients yet can't break out into billionaire status. The truth also is that it is really tough to do so. It is a combination of so many different factors that put someone into the pantheon of Wall Street or business all-stars. Most of it requires the ingredients already mentioned, but there is always an X-factor. Sometimes it's luck, timing, the right idea, or a team surrounding you to make it all happen. Another X-factor could be boldness and successful risk taking. For example, you can go to law school, stay at a law firm for 30 years, and get rich, but it won't be the most fabled and celebrated career as it is an easier road. Unless you are Marty Lipton. He and a few friends started Wachtell, Lipton, Rosen & Katz and in one generation it became one of the most respected law firms in the world.

There is economic rent associated with big success. You can make real money as an investment banker or Wall Street trader but you can't have the major breakout unless you have your own equity and start something. John Paulson, Phil Falcone, Dan Och, Ken Griffin—these are the guys who put themselves out there and succeeded. Bernard Madoff or Marc Dreier—they couldn't get there. Maybe they were missing the brains or the guts or the savvy, but they couldn't settle with it. Dreier, when interviewed by Steve Kroft on *60 Minutes*, said he was "very disappointed" in his life and that at 52, "I wanted my life to be more successful than it was and I saw this as the opportunity to do that in a very obviously, shortsighted, foolish, and selfish way. I had never done anything illegal before . . . but I remember being at a place in my life where I was perhaps desperate to better myself and to make a place for myself."

Philip Delves Broughton wrote in the *Financial Times* that Dreier's great flaw was "envy." He spent so much time in the company of the very rich that he wanted to live like them, whatever it took. He became enveloped in what Broughton called a "quicksand of spending." Dreier himself told the paper that he'd gone to Yale as an undergrad and to Harvard Law, then spent 20 years in several prominent law firms. "I performed well, but I was achieving less satisfaction and recognition than I expected," he told the paper. "Colleagues of mine and certainly clients of mine were doing much better financially and seemingly enjoying more status. By my mid-forties I felt crushed by a sense of underachievement."

So what did he do? He decided to use his influence and write fictitious loans, so he could spend like a fiend, have fancy art on his walls, and feel like a player. This compulsion pushed him over the edge of the law. How could that possibly be worth it? This is a fascinating and dark story. Someone calmer and more in touch with all the great things life had bestowed on him would have been happier with his lot.

Madoff is so clever that he has never publicly talked about what possessed him to hurt so many, especially those who loved and trusted him. To me, that's just further proof that he had the whole thing planned out, knew at some point he would get caught, and he would immediately go into his unremorseful survival plan. It was the recession that uncovered Madoff, not the regulators. He knew how to play them and everybody else. He had the nicest suits, the nicest ties, the nicest houses, boats, and vacations. He was also writing charity checks with other people's money. He was a pillar in the community, and the young regulators swooned and felt intimidated. But I think there is much more to it. I think that he hated, yet envied, his prey—they were wealthier and more successful than he was and were capable of doing it legitimately. He didn't want to be a mediocre, reasonably successful Wall Street guy; that wasn't quite fitting for his ego. He, too, could have been a contender, and for as long as possible on other people's money he was going to be. He is still smirking, laughing at those he hurt, happy at the thought of all the champagne he drank and all the caviar he ate.

We all have pangs of envy, uncertainty, and lack of adequacy in certain situations, but to cross over to the dark side due to these feelings is unforgiveable. No matter what, no amount of consumption is worth being like these despicable people. Keep your ego and envy in check. Make sure you leave your career with honor when it's time to go. Someone who loved you very much likely passed on a legitimate, well-thought-of last name to you. Keep it that way for those in your family's future.

■ ■ ■

There are many undesirables on Wall Street and I have met more than my fair share. It is very easy to be blinded and not think well of people who work in finance, especially today when the industry is the new media punching bag. Yet in the more than 20 years that I have worked on the Street I can tell you that while we have more than our fair share of rogues, we also have some incredible heroes. Here are a few, but there are many others, so if you are reading this and are disappointed that your name isn't here, please know that there simply aren't enough pages for all the many deserved thank-yous. That being said, there are some fantastic Wall Street heroes in the pre- and post-TARP era that you would never hear about.

Now, I am not only telling you about these people so that I can have my soapbox moment and thank them for all that they have taught me. More importantly, in a book dedicated to saying goodbye to Gordon Gekko, I think it is important to say hello to the anti-Gekkos that we never hear about. Perhaps from them the greatest lessons can be learned.

Here are a few:

- **Chris Quackenbush.** Chris was an incredibly smart, energetic guy. He was one of the partners at Sandler O'Neill, an investment bank and trading house that specializes in servicing smaller banks and thrifts. He was a role model for me and someone whom I looked up to. He went to law school, worked at Merrill Lynch, and left a large organization to become part of a start-up. He died in the South Tower of the World Trade Center on September 11, 2001. As I mentioned in Chapter 4, he had been so touched by the Dickens story, he started the Jacob Marley Foundation. He was going to give back. He was a force for charity and good. He built homeless shelters and spent money teaching underprivileged kids how to read. He made sure that the church was taken care of along with just about every charity that touched his heart. He was good to both his undergraduate alma mater, the University of North Carolina, and his law school, NYU. He didn't have any air of superiority about him. In fact, if anything, what I remember most of about him was that he was almost giddy about his success. He worked hard and he was smart, smart enough to know that a lot about his life was luck, too. I can remember him sitting on his waterfront porch overlooking the Manhasset Bay, smoking a cigar and proclaiming himself a "lucky guy."

Chris had the capacity to understand the joy in generosity. He was a great tipper, and caddies on the golf course used to fight over each other to be his guy. Some of the other golfers never got the whole overtipping of the caddy idea. In fact, years ago, I can remember one of them remarking that the overtip actually made the caddie feel inferior, like you were handing them charity or something like that. I didn't see it that way. Chris was sending them a different sort of message: I respect you, I am a lucky dude, I have done very well, and I want you to know that I am not the kind of guy who needs to hoard money. I have enough and maybe this little bit extra will help you and your family. It seemed so simple and pure.

Now I am certain Chris had his flaws—he was human. This passage is not meant to canonize him, nor do I write this to honor him just because he is dead. I write it because he was real. He was charming, caring, and wanted to live life to the absolute fullest.

For him, one of the best days was one of his last days. I had introduced him to Bobby Valentine, who at that time was managing the Mets. Bobby was doing a fund-raiser for Mickey Lione, his old high school coach who had set up a foundation to help the youth of Stamford, Connecticut. Chris came to play golf and then he bid on a pretty nice dream trip. It was to join Bobby in Seattle at the 2001 All-Star Game. Bobby was to manage the National League team and he was going to put Chris and his kids on the field for the home-run derby and all of the fun. Chris won the auction and my friend Doug Romano arranged for him to take his children out there. When he came back, he was so happy and so excited. He did things big and always thought outside the box. I am very proud to have known him. The world was a better place with him as a part of it.

- **Robert Matza.** Bob was the president and chief operating officer of Neuberger Berman, the firm that acquired Oscar Capital in 2001. I remember meeting Bob for the first time. The investment banker who was helping me on the transaction had introduced us at Sparks Steakhouse and we spent over three hours together. I was impressed with his knowledge of and extreme competence in Wall Street's different facets and intricacies.

  When Bob says something he means it. You can do business with him on a handshake. For instance, we had settled on a sale price of Oscar Capital before 9/11 and he stayed committed to buying it (and we adjusted the price in a fair and measured way). He stayed true to his promise of not trying to overmanage us, and never ever stood in my backswing and called out critique. In other words, he allowed me to be me.

  After we moved our team from Oscar to Neuberger, he and Jeff Lane lived up to everything they said they would do. He has uncanny managerial skills and so many gears that he can switch into for different problems and for different sorts of people. He is blunt and truthful but also has a caring side and is willing to apply guidance without being overly dominating.

  He was also capable of dealing with all of the diva money managers that Neuberger had on staff. I learned from him the virtue of dealing with the hypertalented. Gary Kaminsky, arguably one of the best money managers of our generation, would drive Bob cuckoo. Yet Bob loved it and he loved Gary. When Bob sold the firm to Lehman he worked very hard at the transition and wanted to make sure that the decisions that were made were done with both fairness and decency. He is one of my mentors and is on the advisory board of our firm.

- **Robert Castrignano.** On September 14, 2001, I walked into the Sandler O'Neill crisis center when it was becoming clear that the 67 people who worked at the firm and hadn't been heard from since Tuesday, September 11, were likely dead. All 22 people in the Equities Division perished, yet the firm was tasked with the mission to open for stock trading on Monday, September 17, 2001. I went in to see Jimmy Dunne, who was the managing partner of the firm, the best friend of Chris Quackenbush. I handed Jimmy a note with Bob Castrignano's name scribbled on it. I then called Bobby and told him he had to come down to the city from Stamford, Connecticut, and help these guys rebuild their Equities Division. Bob is a patriot and agreed to volunteer and help out for no pay. Jimmy then went to Bob Steel at Goldman Sachs and asked the firm if they would waive their noncompete agreement for Bobby so that he could come in and work full-time. Typical of Bob Steel, he did the right thing and he, along with Goldman Sachs, waived Bobby's contract. Castrignano went to work at Sandler, became a partner there, and in just a little over eight years he has become one of the senior guys in their organization. He is a purposeful man, and someone who makes others believe in themselves. When I met him, he was in charge of the training program in the Equities Division. So many of us owe so much to him.

    Known on Wall Street as "the Coach," if there were a vote on the nicest person ever to have worked at a Wall Street firm, Bobby would be a finalist. While most pack multiple self-serving agendas on Wall Street, Bob clearly has one agenda: to make the people around him better. He is a selfless warrior on Wall Street.

The wayward warriors have often Windexed him. He isn't important enough for them. Yet he is a hero to many.

Having lived in Hong Kong, Tokyo, and traveled throughout the world, Bob has lived a terrific, well-rounded life. Most importantly, he has been a genuine guy who carefully balances his personal life with his professional life. I guess that is why I can still remember the string beans almondine that his mother cooked for us close to 20 years ago.

- **Frank Meyer.** This could possibly be the nicest person I have met on Wall Street. Frank is a legend in the hedge fund business. He was the founder of Glenwood, which he developed into a $7 billion fund of funds before he sold it to the Man Group. One of his most famous acts was when he discovered industry legend and hedge fund superstar Ken Griffin. Ken was a sophomore at Harvard, and Frank seeded him with a million dollars and helped him put together Citadel. Frank has often said that all hedge fund managers have flaws—the trick is to figure out what the flaw is and whether you can help the manager overcome his shortcoming. In Ken's case, according to Frank, his flaw was his age. He was 19 at the time. Frank is the consummate mentor.

  He was raised on Chicago's South Side and had an impulse to give back to his community. Quietly he has helped many children by paying their college tuition and spending his time and energy with them so that they could pursue and realize their dreams. He is soft-spoken, which is uncharacteristic in our business of loudmouths, but his words are more valuable than most. I have often turned to Frank for advice, and while he has a gentle touch he has never been one to mince words. My business and staff have been enriched by having him in our lives.

- **Joseph E. Robert.** Joe is the founder of JER Companies, which is based in the Washington, DC, area. He started his own business and is a major charitable force for young children since the early days of his career. He is a caring and special man. He has been a major significance in my life as he was my first client. In January 2009, I had the opportunity to be with Joe in Davos, Switzerland, at the World Economic Forum. Unfortunately, several days later he was diagnosed with a glioblastoma, which is a malignant brain tumor. Throughout the past year, he has valiantly lived his life to the fullest, never succumbing his spirit to the disease. In 2009, the U.S. Marine Corp honored Joe by making him an honorary Marine. His son has served several tours of duty in Iraq as a Marine, so this is absolutely one of his proudest moments. To express to Joe what he has meant to me, I wrote him a letter that I am including here. There are some great people in the financial services community, and Joe is among the best. Here's the letter I wrote him after Davos.

Joe:

This is a difficult letter for me to write, so I hope you will bear with me as I elucidate some of my thoughts on my relationship with you and the things that I have learned. First off, every once in a while we find people in our lives that are graced with God's most everlasting gift, the love of humanity. It is from people like this that we feel the most intense love of life. Churchill once said that the best among us make "a great effort not to judge human frailty too harshly." The even better among us make it their unilateral mission to help others blindly and without recompense. That, my dear friend, would be you.

I had the good fortune of meeting you in May of 1996. As I recall you were working on selling a business to Goldman. You were in partnership with or about to embark on a partnership with Blackstone but ultimately went with Goldman and eventually sold a piece of your business to Goldman. Upon reflection at the time Goldman was stunned by the upstart Blackstone's success. They paid up for your business not only to make money but to block them. I am sure many have told you how impressive your career is and I am confident that there are those that have fawned over you. For me, I was back then and still am in awe.

I was 32 when we met, with very little money and very big dreams. You, to me, were a fantastic guy, disproving Leo Durocher's rule that nice guys finish last. You were among the nicest and you were excelling. Truly awesome and very inspiring. Today after 20 years of ups and downs in business I see it quite differently. I have met my share of rogues and greedy narcissists, but few and far between have I met people like yourself who have extended to others in such a blunt, nonlinear fashion. You touched my life and have been a terrific role model for me.

Let me remind you of a few things:

1. When Mike Fascitelli introduced us, I flew down and visited you in Tyson's Corner and you immediately agreed to do business with us (Andy and me).

2. You then invited us to participate in several functions at your house in McLean, Virginia, including a fund-raiser for Senator John Warner that Senator Richard Lugar attended.

3. After a short few months, you told the two of us, what are you guys doing? Follow your own dreams and start your own business. Take the risk, live the dream. You didn't just say that—in December of 1996 you gave us $7 million dollars of your own money and became our first client at Oscar Capital. If we were running a pizzeria, you were the first person to buy a pie, and your money was taped to the wall near the oven.

4. We went to France together, and once again you extended your relationships to us—without ever wanting anything. All I can do, Joe, is pay that kindness forward to a whole new group of people, every day.

5. You told us a story about Al Cheechi, where he had come to visit you after doing an LBO of Northwest Airlines with Gary Wilson. The business was flailing. "They had a choice

to either go bankrupt or go public," you politely and charmingly said. They went public.

The most important point to the story was the risk they took and, despite pain and despair, they pulled through. Who among us as entrepreneurs has not felt pain and despair? It was a great story about taking risks to fulfill dreams and embracing fears in a positive way, filled with the excitement of possibility rather than the self-consciousness of failure, and what it brings to us in terms of our self-esteem.

The lesson was about daring, dreaming, and living without fear of failure. And should failure come, not being consumed with it. I mean, after all, why not dream and do? Among our best educators, Lord Tennyson said, "Better to have loved and lost than never to have loved at all," and for the entrepreneur, insert the words *dreamed* and to have *tried*. So satisfying for those who have lurched from the ledge.

You did it. You lurched. You soared and your love for humanity kept you engaged. You did something with your money besides spending it. Your social conscience shined through. I think about your relationships: Quincy Jones, Oprah, Bono, George Tenet, Mark Warner, General Powell—whoever, people got it. They saw who you were. Unpretentious, *real*. They saw you. They felt you. Colorblind. Generations ahead of your time.

You, my dear friend, were gifted with the most precious gift, to see through all: color, income station, role, important and unimportant, it basically didn't matter—driver, shoeshine guy, CEO—to you, all the same. How truly wonderful. See, I have met Oprah (at the Allen conference) and she gets it. So pained through her life, she is blessed with universal empathy. She is loved because she recognizes through most of humanity the love, grace, and general uncertainty. Her gift: I want to make you feel better about your plight. Your gift: The same thing, but you know something else—less fear. No fear, I would say, is inhuman. So I would say just less. I feel your peace. The universe, despite chaos, is ordered enough. And from that you find your peace.

Joe, we all have many regrets about life. Here is one of mine: When our fund/first business started performing badly, I drew away, embarrassed. I missed a wonderful opportunity over the last several years to build a closer relationship with you. When you called last January and figured out a way to meet in Davos I was thrilled.

Even brain tumors have connected us. I serve on the board because of my father and it will be something I work on for the rest of my days because of you and him.

Who knows what God has in store for us? Your whole life you have beat the odds, so my money is on you now. I am here for you and your family and hope that we can pick up where we left off years ago. In fact, I know we already have.

Peace, my friend, and love,

Anthony

Who says there aren't good people on Wall Street? They far out-number the bad people. The trouble is most of them are not searching for the limelight. They are low-key, choosing their charities and good works quietly. The people you meet on the Street come in all shapes and sizes, but what is critical to understand is that the media are spending most of their time focusing on the bad ones. That makes sense to me because it's good for business. But if the industry is to recover its luster, more banks are going to have to do what Jimmy Dunne did: promote the real winners of Wall Street and give them platforms to lead from.

Too often on Wall Street these sorts of people are pooh-poohed as not important enough or ignorant of what it takes to be at the top of the food chain. Blah blah. Enough. It's time to stop being vicious and start be virtuous.

Chapter 9

How to Find Your Fortune without Losing Your Soul

Relax, none of us are getting out alive.

—*Mel Brooks*

admit it: I want it all. Everything. Who doesn't? Oh, and throw in eternal youth, too. I want to be the best, think the deepest thoughts, hang with the most impressive people, eat the most sophisticated food, and, if there are 6.7 billion people on the planet, I want them all (other than the truly evil) to like me. There. I feel better now. Now if only life worked that way.

What's in the way of life working that way? Mostly ourselves.

It was early 2007 when I arrived in the majestic alpine enclave of Davos, Switzerland. Every year, the biggest names and greatest minds in finance, industry, and government from around the world convene on this town—their presence as imposing as the mountain ranges that set up a stunning landscape in *The Sound of Music*—for the World Economic Forum Annual Meeting.

Somehow I was among the luminaries invited to this mind-blowing event. You see, I had gotten here with the help of Michael Dell, who was on the board of the World Economic Forum, the group that hosted the event. Having attended numerous conferences together and done some business together, we'd gotten to know each other well. I was in.

Having familiarized myself with the meeting's program, the first event was a Welcome Reception, which began at 6 P.M. After a long plane ride, I showered, put on my best first-impression clothing, strategically placed my business cards in an easily accessible pocket of my suit, and boarded the shuttle bus to the hotel. I was feeling pretty good about myself.

I arrived at the famous Hotel Belvedere a good half hour before the other attendees started to arrive. It was my first Davos cocktail party—I wanted to look good and be on time. As the ballers started entering the room I felt myself shrink. Something didn't feel right. As I looked around at the gaggles of accomplished billionaires and world leaders, I felt like a Little Leaguer on the field of the all-star game; I was blown away. To my right, there was a social networking entrepreneur and founder of a mega-billion-dollar company; to my left a Nobel Laureate. And get this, the people who surrounded me all seemed at least 10 years younger than I was. Okay, maybe 15 or 20 years younger. Unfortunately, I was more than merely awestruck; I began to feel sick. Thus began a deep case of Davos Envy.

■ ■ ■

What is Davos Envy?

Davos Envy occurs when you look to your left, and then look to your right, and suddenly realize that everyone around you is plainly a lot better than you—more successful, more accomplished, more articulate.

Full of insecurity and pangs of inadequacy, it is accompanied by a severe case of the chills and nervous excitement.

That night, I went back to my little Swiss hotel, flopped on the bed, and pulled the covers over my head. As I tried to close my eyes and go to sleep, the voices in my head were loud and none sounded like Julie Andrews. Instead they sounded like a Fray song continuously questioning me, "Where did I go wrong?" Suddenly, a shaft of enlightenment opened within my feeble brain. As I pulled the covers off my head, it dawned on me that we are all on different paths in life and the biggest gift we can give ourselves is to reject comparisons that make us feel bad about ourselves. Could I be a billionaire? Win a Nobel Prize? Teach at MIT? Maybe—actually, probably not. If I was any of those things, though, I might not have the experiences that are so unique and important to me. I might be too consumed to stay close to my family, too busy to do charity work, and too serious for people to enjoy working at my company (that's not to say that any of those whom I was admiring that evening are any of these things). I began to wonder, what would it take for me, or any of us, to be someone else? It's a game that's probably not worth it.

Now, admitting to you that just a few years ago I felt things that run counter to almost everything I've written in the book is painful. It exposes feelings of which I'm not necessarily proud and puts them in a book that will be printed by the thousands and available for infinite downloads. But remember, I'm not perfect. Like everyone else, I am a work in progress who encounters daily struggles and roadblocks that knock me off the roads I wish to travel. But I strive to pick myself up, be myself, and practice what I preach. That is why I am telling you this story.

You see, that night was an important time in my life because it made me realize that we will always do better in life and be happier if we focus on what we have: our blessings, rather than our lessings. We will never be able to find our fortune unless we stop comparing ourselves to others and embrace who we are.

■■■

Fast-forward to Davos, January 2010.

My good friend Max von Bismarck, director and the head of Investor Industries at the World Economic Forum, gave me the opportunity to speak on a panel. The title of the program was "The Economics of Happiness." During the program, each panelist discussed the importance of personal happiness, and how each individual has a custom definition, yet there are always a few absolutes, like being comfortable in your own skin, happy about the trajectory of life. As I was finishing my remarks, I spoke about Davos Envy and I told the esteemed audience that I wanted to leave them with the following equation:

Less Envy + More Charity and Kindness = Greater Happiness

My friend and former Goldman colleague Frank Brosens humorously pointed out the mathematical flaw with my Davos Envy theory: Not every single person looking to your left and right could actually be doing better than you. He's right (it shows why I'm not on the Nobel list again), but everyone got my point.

In three years, I went from feeling inadequate to thoroughly enjoying myself and participating on a panel in front of the same people whom I highly revered years before. All it took was a hard look in the mirror and a simple attitude adjustment.

You, too, can control the negative feelings that swarm within your mind. It's time to pull off the covers, get out of bed, and snap out of it. Stop being greedy, stop obsessing over your colleague's bonus, stop being jealous of your neighbor's house, stop comparing your life to everyone else.

As the great philosopher Mel Brooks reminds us, we're all going to die. It's trite, perhaps, to say "You can't take it with you," but you really can't. Your greatest legacy is not your wealth, nor your trophy case; it is simply the life you lead and the example you set—how you react to life's difficulties and gracefully share success.

That is the basic idea upon which this book was written and it is the most valuable way for it to conclude—with a road map to finding your true fortune without losing your soul. Remember, wealth is relative—we all have something to share *with* others and something we need *from* others.

So let's toss aside our prior sins and run down some rules to finding your fortune.

Rule 1: You Have to Say Goodbye

Throughout life you'll have to say goodbye to many things, not just Gordon Gekko's greedy mentality. Sometimes it'll be to a loved one who dies, a friend who moves on, a job that you have outgrown, or an idea of who you are and a way in which you have lived.

Life's indignities find us all. Imagine the most beautiful of fashion models at 22 and then picture that same model at 80. Not the same. Same person, sure, but one who is traveling through time in a decaying vessel.

When we're young we do not understand this concept of time acceleration, yet time is relative and it accelerates. The time between 20 and 40 passes by much faster than can be imagined during the smugness of our youth. Think about it: When you graduate from college you think you'll have a lifetime to achieve your lofty professional goals, get rich, have the perfect family, and fly to Paris on a moment's notice. And then suddenly you wake up at the age of 40 and realize that your life isn't what you thought it would be and, worse, you will likely run out of time to fit in all your seemingly unattainable dreams.

Although this realization causes some people to have a midlife crisis, you can prevent it by simply saying goodbye to certain ideas that you had about your life and hello to reality. At times in your life, you'll feel unhappy, unsure, and unsuccessful. All of us do. You can't help it; you are actually wired for it; it's normal. But those of us on a path to finding fortune and happiness must gracefully embrace change and the realities of life.

This sense of clarity, which replaces the uncertainty of youth, is a result of being humbled along the way by the unexpected, unpredictable, and sometimes the unimaginable. I dedicated this book to John F. Iacobucci, a dear friend who was diagnosed with stomach cancer in 1999 and fought valiantly for his life until June 2009. He was brave, dignified, and never lost his faith in all that is wonderful and special in life. When he graduated from college in 1986, I guarantee that he never expected to be leaving life at age 44. Yet he did so with grace and style. He went out on horseback, heading into the sun, just like he promised when he was first diagnosed.

But we don't start out this way. Our view of what is important in life alters as we age or when we are faced with inconceivable situations. As you have read throughout this book, as a young graduate from Tufts, I thought it was important to get a lucrative job as a Wall Street lawyer because it would make me a lot of money and make my parents proud. In my midtwenties, I thought it was important to work at the top financial firm on Wall Street where again I could make tons of money. It wasn't until my thirties that I realized it was important to follow my passion, become an entrepreneur, and mentor young people to do the same. And it was not until I was in my forties that I had the epiphany to just relax into and enjoy my life, to be fully content in my shoes.

For other people, it may take a shorter or longer time to figure it out. Bottom line: There will be loves missed, paths not taken, dreams unfulfilled. We will have to deal with all of these goodbyes, the good and the bad. Only then can we emerge with an enlightened sense of self-awareness.

Rule 2: You Will Be Disappointed—In Others and In Yourself; Forgive First, Analyze Quickly

Over the course of your lifetime you'll have to make many decisions. Decisions. Decisions. Decisions. Some of them will be good ones, others bad ones. You may even make a conscious list of your life expectations, only to find that some will be fulfilled while others will fall to the wayside.

Let's face it: At some point in your life you will be disappointed in yourself or others. Having someone fall short will hurt you; falling short yourself can hurt even more.

Having read fairy tales as kids and watched too many happily-ever-after Disney movies, we start out in an idealistic world dreaming of a life where everything is perfect—the perfect job, the perfect spouse, the perfect kids, and the perfect house. Yet nothing in life is perfect and none of us lead the life we dreamed of growing up—not even those who you think do.

As special as you think you are, circumstances will come up and you will fail and or do the wrong thing and be disappointed in your-self. As I said in Chapter 2, failure happens to the best of us. Don't wallow in your disappointment—forgive yourself and move on. There's a reason a car's rearview mirror is typically only 1/20th the size of the front windshield. It's because you're supposed to spend your time look-ing forward, and metaphorically, that translates to staying focused on what's right in front of you—your present. If the past hurt, release it or rectify it. Forgive yourself, pick yourself up off the ground, and commit to do better.

Similarly, in Dale Carnegie's *How to Stop Worrying and Start Living* (Pocket Books, 1990), I often recite one of his famous passages: "Live in day-tight compartments." What does this mean? Focus on today and tomorrow, not way into the future. He believed that most of our worry stemmed from our obsession with what the future may hold, most of which would likely not come to pass or even be relevant.

Failure and disappointment are a part of growing up and leading a profitable lifestyle. Realize that you will have some regrets in your lifetime. If you want to be successful, you must face these regrets head-on and not wallow in your past. Often, it is through these tough times that we learn how to better adapt to the twists and turns of life so that we can be better prepared for the present.

To this point, I encourage you to take a self-assessment of what you could be doing better. Every so often (less than I should, but more than most), I take a self-assessment and learn what's keeping me from evolving more closely to the person I want to be. It's probably no surprise that the same issues and habits keep popping up. And I bet they are probably the same ones that will keep popping up for you. Throughout our lives, we form habits, both good and bad. What we think are our instincts are frequently just muscle memory taken deep into our existence. Over the next six months, focus on instilling better habits into your life. On a deep level, work at erasing your personal insecurities and building your self-confidence. Self-confidence is habit-based; it grows out of a quiet belief and enough humility to realize no man is isolated whether he succeeds or fails. On a more simplistic level, wake up earlier, set aside time for reading, participate in charitable events, give and commit time for your kids regularly. Our routine is what we make it. So make it a good one.

But what happens when someone else disappoints you? How do you cope with the disappointment that occurs after your boss takes credit for your work or a trusted colleague bad-mouths you to the VP? The trouble arises when our disappointment causes us to get angry at others and, more dangerously, at ourselves. Buddy Hackett, the famous American comedian who thrived in the 1960s, had a great line about anger: "Give it up. While you are angry, the other person is out dancing." We need to learn to control our anger.

As the only one of the seven deadly sins unassociated with self-ishness, anger is one of the most corrosive of all human emotions because it manifests itself in the form of self-denial, revenge, and an unhealthy desire to inflict harm on others or oneself. It rots the body, poisons the mind, and prevents progress. We have to do our best to drop this destructive behavior from our lives. Some of the losers that I have described in this book and have had to deal with have made me angry. At times I have foolishly reacted to them, even though I knew it was wrong—I'm sure you remember my "double chin" remark from

Chapter 4. We are all fallible and human. Waking up, though, every day and committing to be better and more forgiving will help you achieve true wealth and success.

How you do it—dealing directly with the target of your anger or quietly praying it away—varies but the result is nearly universal. It releases us from reliving pain and it gives us the best chance we have to grow into the best version of ourselves.

Force forgiveness into your heart. Since it is against all the survival instincts of your body, this is a very hard thing to do, but just as the anger doesn't hurt anybody but yourself, forgiving somebody is a very powerful health tonic.

Count your blessings, not regrets. Move forward.

Rule 3: Keep Your Ego in Check

In order to find your fortune you'll also need to keep your ego in check and project self-awareness without being too humble or too arrogant. There's a fine line between arrogance and humility. To me, arrogance is a person who spends the first 20 minutes in your presence trying to define themselves as superior to you. The arrogant man thinks, "I have more dough, better art, better homes; I am smarter, my business is better, and so are my vacations and family members." By contrast, humility is the person who appears inept or inexperienced at handling the twists and turns of life. Alternatively, this person may reek of false modesty and in actuality be a wolf disguised in sheep's clothing.

In order to succeed, it is important to balance these traits. Picture this balance like a level—you know, the rectangular thing that you use to hang a picture on wall. Well, you represent the tiny bubble that has to fit in between the two lines, which represent humility and arrogance. If the bubble lands in the middle, that's the definition of acceptable self-confidence. All is well.

If the bubble is leaning toward the arrogance line, make sure you are still behaving consistently with your values and not thrown off by the greed–envy downward cycle. Don't let your pride get in the way of your success. Put your ego in a jar and put it on a shelf behind you. If you subordinate yourself to the betterment of the team, everybody wins.

Don't let your ego prevent you from seeking out a mentor or learning from others. People who think they are too smart, too experienced, or too proud find themselves on the path of self-destruction because they are constantly trying to prove that they are right at all costs. Blinded by their relative amounts of certainty, they often fail—just ask some of the guys who facilitated the financial crisis of 2008. Surround yourself with great people who are willing to call you out and guide you from their own experience. Listen to the advice of trusted mentors. Find people who can help you find yourself.

On the flip side, it's okay to toot your horn a little. People need to know that you're aware of your accomplishments and abilities and are confident in making decisions. Self-doubt creates self-consciousness and breeds insecurity, which often creates overcompensation. This is a recipe that we need to try to avoid. Relax, put your ego in check, and be the best that you can be.

Rule 4: Be Yourself and Have Fun

I often think that the most charismatic people get that way from just being themselves and not conforming to a corporate culture that is at odds with who they are as individuals. They can often lighten a room with their originality and nonconformity, usually by saying something that is very true, but others feel uncomfortable saying or hearing. These types of people encourage an intellectually challenging culture that enables others to better refine their theories and improve their future actions.

As an ambitious person, you must always be true to yourself. Each of us has been given a gift; we each have a unique personality fingerprint. It's best to get comfortable with all of your unique personality traits and not force too many changes—especially for the sake of money. If you try to hide who you are, you will become so stifled that all the money in the world won't erase your internal discontent and unhappiness.

Sure, an established corporate culture is important for a company's long-term success and provides its employees with a sense of universal ethics, but we all know when conformity is too much. Don't fall prey to peer pressure or hide who you are just to impress others or receive a hefty paycheck. Trust me, there will come a point where your unique, God-given gifts will come in handy. If you let your personality wither away, you'll be crippled at crunch time. Be original. If you fail, it'll be on your own terms. If you succeed, then you'll find a level of self-confidence for which there is no substitute.

To this point, don't take life too seriously. A sense of humor goes a long way; it attracts people. And it's okay to have one as it relates to your shortcomings, too. Smile. It will change the way people look at you. Saying something with a smile may not change what you are saying, but it might change its meaning.

Make jokes? Have fun? Smile?

Really?

In a book about achieving wealth?

Absolutely. What else can you do? Be playful, self-deprecating, self-assured, and affable to those around you. If you're a boss, it is a great leveler, a great way to relate to people. If you're not a boss, it can be a way to lead, to teach and build camaraderie.

You can even use humor and playtime to support your work efforts. For instance, a friend of mine who is a newspaper editor often walks through his troops at deadline time—the most anxious part of the day—with a Nerf pistol, firing point-blank at those who haven't filed their stories. Sure, this is a fun activity that takes the edge off of his staff, but it also gets the point across: File your story . . . or be shot.

Don't get me wrong, fun isn't always a tool for business. However, it's crucial in allowing you to enjoy your life and get distance from serious issues that are negatively impacting your well-being or performance.

Rule 5: Rejoice in the Success of Others

Someone you know will do spectacular things: It might be you, might be your brother or sister or best friend or classmate. They might become president, a movie star, a star athlete, a millionaire, or a war hero. As I have said throughout this book, you must be the person who cheers on the success of others and rejoices in their achievements. Embrace it.

It doesn't take away from your own achievements or diminish your accomplishments if you have the maturity and professionalism to be a team player. Remember, you can find your place in the world and be collegial with those you meet along the way—who likely are people you will often want or need to be around in the future. The big trick in life is figuring out your need for personal glory and balancing it with your ability to get along within your team and be a contributing member.

The best among us can drop our envy and celebrate the successes of our friends. Don't compare or be bitter. Hit the emotional override button and know that there is enough success and bounty in life for everybody. We all have different equipment, different life experiences, different skills, and different origins that make us . . . different. What a gift to teach children: Celebrate the successes of your friends. Drop the atavistic social Darwinism and become sublime. Be joyful for the joy of others.

Chances are, though, that you will feel diminished by someone's good fortune, accomplishments, or success. Your ability to handle these feelings is crucial; your survival and quality of life depend on it.

Ever hear of Joe P. Kennedy Jr.? He was JFK's older brother.

In *The Kennedy Legacy: Jack, Bobby and Ted and a Family Dream Fulfilled* (Palgrave Macmillan, 2009), author Vincent Bzdek chronicles the family's accomplishments and misfortunes and discusses the competitive relationship among the eight Kennedy children, especially the four boys. Bzdek theorizes that Joe Jr. might have died because of his unique relationship with brother Jack.

According to a *USA Today* review of the book:

Bzdek says the rivalry extended to the brothers' World War II exploits and may have led to Joe Jr.'s death.

The trigger was a night in August 1943, when a Japanese warship sliced in half a Navy Patrol Torpedo boat commanded by Jack. Ten of the 12 men on board the PT-109 survived the ordeal, in large part because of Jack's decisions.

Jack returned to a hero's welcome.[*]

According to Bzdek, while everyone was downstairs celebrating Jack's courage, a friend claims that he found Joe Jr. crying upstairs in his room. As a result, "Joe, a naval aviator, started volunteering for riskier and riskier missions even after he was supposed to come home," Bzdek says. "He wanted to show his courage and really outshine his brother."

In 1944, Joe volunteered for a dangerous mission over France. With his plane loaded with explosives, it accidentally detonated and he died. Joe Jr. was supposed "to be the family's first political star," but he was now gone.

Although this seems to be an extreme instance, I have painfully watched people not deal well with the success of others. Don't let it be you.

Comparatively, you should also be there for your boss or colleagues when they fail or life hands them misfortune. Although you may be surprised by the success of some of your colleagues and peers, you will be even more surprised by the unraveling of others. Make sure you are good to both types of people. Be the type of person who offers to buy your down-and-out friend a drink. Not only will your friend appreciate it, if he is capable and resilient he will rise again . . . and you'll be there with him. Most people in that situation do not forget the kindness

---

[*]Jill Lawrence, "Youngest Son Reflected Kennedys' Ambition, Foibles," *USA Today*, August 26, 2009.

shown when they are vulnerable and have little else but their friendship to offer. After all, these things move in cycles, so nobody—not even you—stays on top or on the bottom for long.

Rule 6: Give

In Michael Lewis's *The Blind Side* (W. W. Norton & Company, 2006), a white upper-class family takes in an underprivileged African-American kid and makes him part of their family. As a stellar football player, they help him fulfill his potential both on and off the playing field. Although he eventually becomes the first-round NFL draft pick for the Baltimore Ravens, the success in this story is found in its giving and charitable nature.

Throughout this book, I have emphasized the importance of giving—the incredible feeling of trying to lift up another person's soul through charitable donations or the giving of your time. We tingle when we can extend ourselves to someone—like there's an instinct saying that it is indeed the best part of us making itself visible.

My prescription for finding your fortune while not losing your soul: Give time and money to causes you believe in, and teach others who can benefit from your wisdom and experience. One of the best parts of having money is being able to give it to other people. It's another of those rare clichés that are true: It is actually better to give than to receive.

If you are unable to give a monetary donation because of your income level and everyday expenses, then give your time by volunteering. Whether it is as the coach of your child's basketball team, as the event coordinator of a Cancer Society benefit, or as an adviser in an underprivileged kids' program, your time can make the difference in a person's life. Of the different volunteer efforts that I participate in, the Student Sponsorship Program has a special place in my heart. In this program, I met Errol Smalls, a 13-year-old boy who lived in the South Bronx, and I helped him pay his tuition to the Monsignor Scanlon High School. There he was taught by a passionate group of nuns, other clergy, and lay teachers. He graduated from high school and went on to college to learn information technology and work in that sector. I learned more from Errol than he could learn from me.

Giving shouldn't stop on the individual level. We as a society can lift each other up. Think of the global response to the Haitian earthquake or to the tsunami in Southeast Asia. We care, even about people and nations with which we are unfamiliar.

Rule 7: Target Success

Plan. Flow. Adapt. Plan. Flow. Compromise. Adapt. Plan—all the while trying to execute and strive for success. With quiet determination, grit, hard work, and effort, good things will happen regardless of what is going on in the economy. As you have read, I started as a young kid in a Camaro, became an investment banker in the Goldman Sachs Real Estate Corporate Finance Department, and am now a founding partner of a global hedge fund seeding and fund-of-funds business. If you asked me how I got here from there, I'd tell you it was a combination of twists and turns: nothing absolute, no bright star guiding me, just life flowing. Along the way, I learned that when you plan, God laughs. Be flexible—we all have to brace for the impact of the unexpected, while targeting success.

In *Lincoln Speaks to Leaders*, by Gene Griessman and Pat Williams (Elevate, 2009), the authors discuss Lincoln's will to succeed and his many setbacks. In a letter that Lincoln wrote to a young man, he said:

> I know not how to aid you, save in the assurance of one of
> mature age, and much severe experience, that you cannot fail,
> if you resolutely determine that you will not.

Essentially, Lincoln was telling his audience that you will never fail if you believe that you will succeed. When you hit a roadblock, like the one I experienced that night in Davos in 2007 or when I was fired from my first job at Goldman Sachs, think about Lincoln's resolve and the clarity of his words.

To this point, don't b.s. yourself. We all have a persona that we project to the outside world. If you start to truly believe the embellished story of your life that you created, you will be knocked down. You have to stay vigilant about your sensibilities and ego. Buy a great suit and exude confidence, but make a checklist in your quiet times of things that have to be fixed and spots where you got lucky. You'll be the better for it.

Remember, the best version of you is the way you define yourself when you are daydreaming; when your self-consciousness is low, and your self-awareness is high; when it dawns on you that this is your life and it's a pretty good one; when the bellyaching and whining stop; when you are proud to say who you are.

■■■

Yes, it's true, I want it all—but not at the expense of staying true to myself and living a happy life. Although I have been fortunate enough to eat off the wealth menu and afford some of the greater material luxuries in life, no amount of money would make me compromise who I am.

Sure, I respect those who have climbed up the material mountain (and many of us may even be those hikers), but you have to ask yourself about the value of it all. Greed will force a compromise of our principles; it makes you do things you don't want to do. Sorry Gekko, but greed *isn't* good—look where it landed you. And to all the Gekkos out there who contributed to the financial crisis, ask yourself, was it worth it? All the money in the world, but now society's pariahs? Is that a good trade? We are all in it together, and the rest of us are on to you.

It's time to dial it down a notch and give something back. The best medicine: Be greedy about doing what you enjoy. Once you are, the money and prestige will inevitably come.

Passion and self-awareness, not money and material possessions, are the key ingredients to leading a rich and profitable life. Push yourself to feel a deep, intense, enthusiastic commitment to everything that you do, and react positively to life's twists and turns. And if you are not passionate about what you are doing, think about doing something else.

We all start out with high expectations. We believe that we are going to provide a greater life for our kids than our parents gave us and that we'll be able to correct their sins. We believe that we are going to have it all and be different—we aren't going to be a slave to our job, wear the wingtips, or shop at Ann Taylor. We are going to be able to get to the top of Maslow's pyramid of self-actualization very quickly. So confident and smug—then life hits us and we are in the abyss with nothing looking back at us.

It is at that moment that we have to decide our path. Drive around the neighborhood and look at the houses bigger than your own with bitterness, or feel the enlightenment of having the gift of life and all of its ups and downs. If you can bring yourself over the reality line, passing through the Disney happily-ever-after portal, and still love life, then you'll have found your fortune and all that is fortunate.

Further Reading

In Chapter 5, I discussed the importance of reading as a means to acquire knowledge and expand your existing ideology. I have a love for reading that I try to share with my colleagues, mentees, young entrepreneurs, and children. Here are a few books that had an incredible influence on me and that I encourage you to read:

- *The Odyssey* by Homer (Robert Fagles translation)
- *Augustus: The Life of Rome's First Emperor* by Anthony Everitt
- *How to Stop Worrying and Start Living* by Dale Carnegie
- *Lincoln at Gettysburg* by Garry Wills
- *The Gold Coast* by Nelson DeMille
- *Churchill* by Roy Jenkins
- *A Peace to End All Peace* by David Fromkin
- *From Shtetl to Suburbia* by Sol Gittleman
- *The Psychology of Winning* by Denis Waitley
- *Learned Optimism* by Martin Seligman
- *The Last Lion: Winston Spencer Churchill: Alone 1932–1940* by William Manchester

Now you may be wondering why I would recommend these books in a business narrative about finding your fortune and leading a profitable life. The truth is that you cannot financially or professionally succeed unless you instill positive habits in your life and stay true to yourself. In their own unique ways, these books will help you learn how to develop the habits of a winner, confront adversity, rise from failure, and take solace in your personal journey.

Acknowledgments

There have been so many people throughout my life from whom I have learned, many of whom I mentioned in this book, but there are countless others who have guided and mentored me throughout my journey. Although there aren't enough pages in the book to list all of their names, I want all of them to know how grateful I am. To name a few, I want to thank Jack Shepherd and Kevin Wang, who helped me get my first job at Goldman Sachs; Richard Glanas, Dick Rogoff, and David Henle; Ed Spiegel, who left us too early; Ken Brody, Tony Lauto, Josephine Linden, Richard Glanas, Geoff Boisi, David Darst, John Watras, Robert Sechan, Brian Hull, Greg Fleming, Bob McCann, and Bob Castrignano. Also Moses Tsang, Andrew K. Boszhardt Jr., Jeffrey B. Lane, Scott Prince, Kenneth G. Langone, Herbert A. Allen III, Larry Bacow, Jim Stern, Nathan Gantcher, and Richard DiVenuto.

I also want to thank all the people who encouraged me to write this book and those who took a look at the early drafts and helped me make the manuscript better. Here are a few shout-outs: Thank you to the members of my staff at SkyBridge, in particular Sue Ponce, Deidre Ball, Minna Urrey, and my partner, Victor Oviedo, who made many insightful comments; my mentors, Mike Fascitelli and Bob Matza, for reading the early chapters and offering their insight; all of the various members of the Scaramucci family, the production staff of

Wall Street: Money Never Sleeps, including Oliver Stone, Eric Kopeloff, Ed and Annie Pressman, Celia Costas, Antoine Douaihy, Amanda Crisses, Amy Draughn, Morgan Marling, and of course Josh Brolin and Shia LaBeouf. It was so gratifying to have the opportunity to work with you.

And my deep thanks to the two people who had the biggest impact on the text: Dan Colarusso, who was absolutely brilliant at getting the concepts I was trying to address; and lastly and most importantly Kelly O'Connor, who worked tirelessly on this project and went far above the call of duty to edit my writing and force me to be more clear, but always allowed me to have my voice. She is a fantastic editor and writer.

It would be impossible to express my gratitude to everyone who has helped me. All I can say is thank you and I intend to do my best to pay it forward.

ANTHONY SCARAMUCCI

New York, New York
April 2010

About the Author

Anthony Scaramucci is the founder and managing partner of Sky-Bridge Capital LLC. Focused on partnering with emerging managers, the fund now has seven managers and $4.4 billion in assets. Prior to opening SkyBridge, Mr. Scaramucci was a partner and co-founder of Oscar Capital Management LLC, where he oversaw compliance and research for four hedge funds and separately managed accounts with over $1 billion in assets. In 2001, Oscar Capital was sold to Neuberger Berman LLC. As managing director of Neuberger Berman/Lehman Brothers from 2003 to 2005, Mr. Scaramucci served on the investment committee of Neuberger's Premier Portfolio and worked on the Neuberger Berman/Lehman integration team. From 1989 to 1996, he was at Goldman Sachs & Co., where in 1993 he became a vice president in Private Wealth Management.

Mr. Scaramucci earned a BA in economics from Tufts University in 1986, where he graduated summa cum laude and was a member of the Phi Beta Kappa society. In 1989, he graduated with a JD from Harvard Law School. He is a board member of the Lymphoma Foundation and the Brain Tumor Foundation, on the board of overseers for the School of Arts and Sciences at Tufts University, and a member of the NYC Financial Services Advisory Committee. Mr. Scaramucci is also a frequent commentator on CNBC, FOX Business, and Bloomberg TV and was one of the technical advisers on the *Wall Street* sequel, *Wall Street: Money Never Sleeps*.

Index